MW00948160

DON'T BURY ME
IN A TUXEDO

To my dear 511!!

Thanks for being a
nice part of my life!

Always,!

"Fia"

DON'T BURY ME
IN A TUXEDO

Memoirs of a Trumpet Player

Daryl "Flea" Campbell

Copyright © 2008 by Daryl "Flea" Campbell.

Library of Congress Control Number: 2008908203
ISBN: Hardcover   978-1-4363-7044-8
                   Softcover   978-1-4363-7043-1

All rights reserved. No part of this book may be reproduced or transmitted in any form
or by any means, electronic or mechanical, including photocopying, recording, or by
any information storage and retrieval system, without permission in writing from the
copyright owner.

This book was printed in the United States of America.

To order additional copies of this book, contact:
Xlibris Corporation
1-888-795-4274
www.Xlibris.com
Orders@Xlibris.com
42793

CONTENTS

Foreword 9
Preface 11

Chapter One   "Yes Sir, That's My Baby" 13
Chapter Two   "I've Got a Pocket Full
                   of Dreams"/"That's a Plenty" 16
Chapter Three   "Deep Purple" 19
Chapter Four   "Tweedin' Kirby Watson" 25
Chapter Five   On the Boardwalk in Atlantic City 28
Chapter Six   "Off We Go into the Wild Blue Yonder" 32
Chapter Seven   "If the Japs Only Knew What
                   Our Arranging Staff Could Do!" 34
Chapter Eight   "All That Glitters Is Not Gold" 41
Chapter Nine   The Peppy Pirates/
                   "Open the Door, Richard" 47
Chapter Ten   "Stardreams" and "In Flew the Flea" 53
Chapter Eleven   "I'm Getting Sentimental
                   over You" (First Chorus) 61
Chapter Twelve   "Getting Sentimental
                   over You" (Second Chorus) 69
Chapter Thirteen   Cuba/Copa 80
Chapter Fourteen   "Getting Sentimental
                   over You" (Out Chorus) 84
Chapter Fifteen   Jingles/Jungle 101
Chapter Sixteen   The King of Swing 107
Chapter Seventeen Moon over Miami 110
Chapter Eighteen   A Medley of Bob Crosby, Xavier Cugat,
                   Liberace, Vaughn Monroe, Wayne King 116
Chapter Nineteen   Top of the World....................................123
Chapter Twenty   Jukebox Saturday Night.......................128
Chapter Twenty-One California, Here I Come 132
Chapter Twenty-Two The Polish Prince...............................137

Chapter Twenty-Three   The Second Time Around 153
Chapter Twenty-Four   What a Difference a Day (Job) Makes! 156
Chapter Twenty-Five   On the Road Again..165
Chapter Twenty-Six   Myrtle Beach, South Carolina
                       (The Redneck Riviera) (Part One) 169
Chapter Twenty-Seven   The City of Light 171
Chapter Twenty-Eight   On the Road Again . . . Again.......................173
Chapter Twenty-Nine   The Redneck Riviera (Part Two) 175
Chapter Thirty   In the Loop (and the Front Seat) 178
Chapter Thirty-One   Closing Theme...182

Index 187

For my children,

Darla, Daryl, Juda Lynn;

my grandson Zachary;

my best friend Leonore;

and every guy and gal who ever shared a bandstand with me

Special thanks to Shirley Alberti for her incisive and helpful editing.

Cover design by . . . Zach Campbell and Ben Pruitt

FOREWORD

When Flea asked me to write something for his book, my head was crowded with fifty years of memories. What do I say about this man? About our friendship, our love affair, our children, and our music. What can possibly encompass in a few words—all of the emotions of a lifetime shared with another soul? So I sat down, said a little prayer, and waited for the words to come.

This is the story of a little boy with a dream. A dream that pretty much has come true. He made it happen and at age eighty-four is still playing his music in a most professional way. The sad part is—most of this music no longer exists. It's like watching someone you love die slowly.

Edwin Daryl "Flea" Campbell and I have known each other for fifty-eight years. Through five marriages between us, illness—cancer, heart disease, problems with our kids, we are still standing tall. Even people we know don't really understand our relationship.

This book is about *life*, not just about music. Flea has always had a wonderful sense of humor. He could always make me laugh. You'll laugh too at some of the crazy situations he has lived through.

I'm proud of my friend, I'm proud to be his friend, and I'm so proud that he wrote this book! We didn't stay married, but we've always been there for each other because that's what life and love and friendship is all about.

L. R.

PREFACE

On the morning of November 26, 1956, Lynn Roberts, my wife at the time, and I had just finished breakfast in our Astoria, Long Island, apartment when the phone rang.

It was a drummer friend of mine that I had worked with at the Copacabana. He said, "Gee, Flea, I sure was sorry to hear about what happened with Tommy." I thought he was talking about an incident that happened the previous Saturday night in the Café Rouge of the Statler Hotel when Lynn and Tommy had somewhat of an argument on the bandstand, and Tommy figured he could end it by saying, "If you don't like the way I run things you can leave . . ." which is just what she did: she got up and walked off the bandstand.

I said to my friend, "Oh, that's nothing, it's happened before, it will all blow over." He sounded puzzled when he said, "Do you have your television on?" I answered, "No." He said, "You better put it on." I turned to Lynn and said, "Honey, turn on the TV."

Well, there it was, full coverage with all the details of how Tommy Dorsey had been found dead that morning in his home in Greenwich, Connecticut.

We were both shocked; we couldn't believe that a fifty-three year-old man so full of life could be gone.

Three days later, we both attended Tommy's funeral service at Frank Campbell's Funeral Parlor on Madison Avenue in Manhattan. There were about three hundred people in attendance, mostly from the music business. It felt like the twilight zone to me. Especially when Tommy's wife, threw herself on his coffin screaming, "Oh, Tom, my sweet Tom." It seemed ludicrous knowing that two days before they both would have been in court going through a nasty divorce.

Just then the organ player began to play Tommy's theme song "I'm Getting Sentimental over You" with all the wrong chord changes! Every guy in the band turned his head toward the casket, fully expecting Tommy to sit up and say, "Jesus Christ! If there's a stiff around, he'll wind up on my payroll." One of his favorite expressions.

As I sat there watching all this go on, I thought to myself, *How did I get here?*

I am just a month shy of my eighty-fourth birthday, and I now have time to reflect on the events of my life, so I thought it might be fun to share some of them with you.

I guess it all began when . . .

CHAPTER ONE

"Yes Sir, That's My Baby"

I was born Edwin Daryl Campbell on August 25, 1924, in East Conemaugh, Pennsylvania, a small coal-dust-covered suburb of Johnstown. My parents, Chester Homer Campbell and Catherine Wentz Campbell, were hardly more than children themselves at that time. My father was seventeen, my mother sixteen.

Times were tough for the young couple, so we moved in with an aunt Kate and uncle Jack who had helped raise my mother. My father was offered a job in Illinois, and they couldn't figure how they could take me with them until they got settled, so my aunt, actually my great-aunt, said, "You kids go ahead and leave Daryl with us, we'll take care of him."

I don't know how it happened, but somehow we all wound up moving to Pittsburgh.

That first year we all lived together for a short time, but when my aunt and uncle moved into their own apartment, they took me with them. They never had any children of their own, so I guess they liked having me around.

My aunt could be domineering, and my parents being so young didn't know how to deal with her, so they just went along with it.

My uncle Jack was a kind, gentle man, and I loved him very much. He was a freight conductor on the Pennsylvania Railroad, earning a grand total of $30 a week!

I never wanted for anything, even though sometimes dinner consisted of white bread smothered with brown gravy. We called it gravy bites! I honestly had a very happy childhood.

We had a tall Victrola that you had to wind up in order to play records. As the story goes, when I was about three years old and not tall enough to reach the handle, I would jump up and down and holler until someone came and wound it for me, and the record I would sing along with was "Yes Sir, That's My Baby." Believe it or not, I still remember all the lyrics!

My uncle Jack had a very tough job. Many nights, in the freezing cold, he would be out walking the tops of boxcars. Also, there were times when he would be laid off from work, and we would have to move in with my parents; but whenever he got back to work and they moved out, I went with my aunt and uncle.

We never lived very far from my parents, never more than four or five blocks, so I saw them quite often.

By the time I was eight, I had two new brothers, Homer Ronald and Dana Jack. They grew up with my parents, but I remained with my aunt and uncle. Despite this odd arrangement, we were very close. We did all the things young boys do, play baseball, build model airplanes, and play cowboys and Indians.

The only thing I really hated about living in Pittsburgh was the winters. They were bitter cold, and sometimes the snow could be well over the roof of a car. The apartment we lived in had no central heat. All we had were open-flame gas heaters in each room. To keep the cost down, the only one that was lighted in the morning was the one in the dining room. The windows in my bedroom had an inch thick ice on the inside panes. On school days, I had to jump out of bed, run into the dining room, and hold my corduroy knickers in front of the heater to thaw them out! I secretly promised myself that when I was able, I would never live in a cold climate again.

My uncle Jack had three friends that he worked with on the railroad, and they rented a house in Pardee, Pennsylvania, in the Bald Eagle Valley. They each got to choose two weeks out of the summer to spend there with their families. We called it the fishing camp because of the creek that ran behind the house, where we spent hours fishing for catfish and sunfish, and it was also our swimming hole. Railroad tracks ran right through our front yard, where the local train traveled between Sunbury and Bellefonte, back and forth twice a day. This house had absolutely no modern conveniences, no electricity, no running water, and the mattresses we slept on were stuffed with straw. We pumped water from the well in the yard, and if we needed hot water, we had to heat it on an old iron stove. At night, the only light we had was from kerosene lanterns. After the first few days, we had huge lumps all over from mosquito bites, which my aunt took care of by pouring rubbing alcohol on our heads! The toilet was a two-holer outhouse, which could be rather pungent on a hot day!

There were other kids that lived there; they were real hillbillies. They didn't wear shoes, so the soles of their feet were like leather. They wore overalls and no underwear! But we all had a lot of fun together.

The big entertainment was every Saturday night when we all went up to the CCC (Civilian Conservation Corps) camp where they showed an outdoor movie. It was always a Gene Autry movie (my favorite was Tom Mix), and we loved those two weeks every summer going to fishing camp.

CHAPTER TWO

"I've Got a Pocket Full of Dreams"/ "That's a Plenty"

My mother played the piano and the flute, never professionally, but I'm sure any musical talent I have I inherited from her. My father played the cornet in high school, but I didn't find that out until much later.

My mother had a secret desire to be in show business; so when I was about twelve, she decided that she, my two brothers, and I should learn to tap dance. Our act was to be known as the Dancing Campbells.

We started taking lessons at the Jack Barry dance studio on the second floor of an old building on Stanwick Street in downtown Pittsburgh. It was a long room with tall mirrors along one wall, an old upright piano, and a large dance mat in front of the mirrors, so you could watch yourself as you learned the dance steps. A very nice lady by the name of Ruth played the piano while accompanying us as we learned the routines.

I really liked to tap dance, and it came very easily to me because I picked up on the rhythmic patterns of the taps. My mother and my brother Ronnie had to work at it a lot harder, so I had to sit by and wait for them to learn the steps. My little brother Jack was so cute it didn't matter what he did. My mother bought a large dance mat and put it in the basement. I was going to a different school than my brothers, so every day after school, I had to go to their house so that we could practice.

We learned four or five different routines, and my mother made all of our costumes. We had a bellboy number with suits made out of red satin with brass buttons, a cowboy number complete with leather chaps and Stetson hats, a Chinese number with outfits made out of blue and gold brocade, and an outfit with large blue and white stripes, floppy red ties, and little red caps! That was our big number done to an old Dixieland tune "That's a Plenty." (I now play that tune as part of the Clambake Seven with Buddy Morrow and the Tommy Dorsey Orchestra.)

One day, a guy came to the dance studio demonstrating a new home recording outfit, and for ten bucks, he would make a record for you. Well, at that time, I had a high soprano voice, so my mother had me sing "I've Got a Pocket Full of Dreams" and do a tap routine. (I still have that record around somewhere!) My brother Ronnie tells me he and I did a routine on "Lulu's Back in Town." (It must have been pretty bad because I don't remember it at all!) We actually started to get some engagements around Pittsburgh, mostly local political rallies, kiddy shows at the Enright Theater, and once in awhile a show at the Sons of Italy hall. I always looked forward to those shows because the people were so warm and friendly, and the food was always great! (I still love pasta!)

I have always felt comfortable in the company of Italians. As the cliché goes, some of my closest friends have been Italian. Charlie Russo, Buddy Yannon (Iannone) from the Charlie Spivak band; Vinnie Carbone, one of Tommy Dorsey's managers (who actually found Tommy Dorsey the morning he died), Joe Long (Skiavo), a fine saxophone player in Myrtle Beach, who made me an honorary Italian when he found out I could order spaghetti and meatballs in Italian. In 1939, my mother sent a letter to the *Major Bowes Amateur Hour*, a very popular radio show at that time, inquiring about an audition. Auditions were held in New York City, and if you wanted to travel there, at your own expense of course, you could try out. Well, we did. We passed the audition and was scheduled to be on the show that following Sunday!

Because of a New York child labor law, my two younger brothers were not permitted to be on the show. One had to be at least twelve years old; so just the two of us, my mother and I did our "That's a Plenty" routine. We didn't win, we came in third!

Anyone who listened to the *Major Bowes Amateur Hour* on radio thought that the kindly old man was standing right next to you and talking to you when in actuality, the crusty old bastard sat in a glass-enclosed booth in the middle of the theater and talked to you over a loudspeaker. We never got within one hundred feet of him! We stayed in New York for a couple more days and took in the 1939 New York World's Fair and the Empire State Building. My mother also took me to the Capitol Theatre to see the *Wizard of Oz,* and the live stage show featured Judy Garland and

Mickey Rooney. (Eleven years later, I played at the Capitol Theatre with the Charlie Spivak Orchestra!)

As I said before, I really liked to tap dance, and I have always admired great dancers like Fred Astaire, Gene Kelly, Sammy Davis Jr., and Gregory Hines. I used to love to play for an act called the Four Step Brothers; they were great dancers. That was just about the end of the Dancing Campbells. I think my father put the kibosh on any of Mother's future thoughts about show business. Although, when they both retired to Florida because of my father's health, she became very active despite several strokes in the Little Theatre in Daytona Beach. Acting, painting the scenery, and once again making costumes until she passed away in 1972. Bless her!

CHAPTER THREE

"Deep Purple"

I did pretty well in grade school and graduated in June 1938.

I had a friend that was in the same Boy Scout troop that I was in, and he had a set of drums at his house. Sometimes, after school, I would go there, and he would let me fool around with his drum set. I told my aunt I thought I would like to learn to play the drums; however, a drum set cost about $500, and there was no way my aunt and uncle could afford that.

In those days, if you wanted to learn to play an instrument, you could call the local store, and they would send a salesman out to demonstrate it for you.

My aunt called and had them send out a Hawaiian guitar. The guy came with the guitar and the beginner's book. You had to hold it on your lap, strum it with a pick, and with your left hand, hold a small metal bar that you moved back and forth over the strings to get that tinny Hawaiian sound.

I completed the beginner's book in about an hour and had absolutely no interest in the Hawaiian guitar.

Not to be discouraged, the salesman said, "How about if I bring you a trumpet next week?" I said, "Okay."

Sure enough, he showed up with this shiny silver horn in a black leather case with bright red plush lining. I thought it was beautiful!

He tried to show me how to blow into the mouthpiece to get a sound, but when I tried it, all that came out was air. He assured me that in a little while, I would be able to hang it from the ceiling on a string and, without holding it with my hands, play notes. (To this day I haven't tried it!) Well, that's what I wanted, the trumpet, so my aunt and uncle bought it for me.

It was a Conn Cavalier that cost $65. They paid five bucks a week until it was paid off.

Pretty soon, I was able to get a decent sound out of it, so I taught myself to play songs as long as they didn't go above a middle C on the horn. Of course, I couldn't read music, and I couldn't write down notes, so I wrote down the fingerings of the valves such as 1 for the first valve, 1-2 if those two valves were held down together, 3-2-3, etc. The letter *O* meant open, no valves. One song that worked great that way was "Over the Rainbow." All I had to do was match up the rhythm with the fingerings, and I could play the song. My friend with the drums and I would play at our Scout meetings. (I'd love to hear that now!)

That fall, I entered Peabody High School as a freshman and signed up for beginners' band. As I said before, I couldn't read music, and then one day, suddenly, I could. It happened just like that, I can't explain it. Actually I became a very proficient reader. I even taught myself to read two bars ahead while playing. (Charlie Shavers, the great black trumpet player once remarked, "This guy could read fly shit!")

By my sophomore year, I was in the marching band and the concert band. One day, we all went to the auditorium to hear a dance band from a rival high school, and when I heard that sound, something happened! I had never felt anything like it before! A whole new world opened up before me.

My two best friends, Clyde Costly and Bob Greene, were both trumpet players. We started to learn about the big bands and that kind of music.

About that time, our music teacher, Mr. Wallace Frost, said he wanted to start a rhumba band, and the three of us would be the trumpet section. Clyde played first trumpet because he could hit a high D!

It went fine for a while, but we didn't want to play rhumbas; we wanted to play swing! He finally bought us some big band arrangements such as Glenn Miller's "Chattanooga Choo Choo."

We would go to the local record store to hear Harry James's latest record. In those days, you could take the record into a booth and listen to it to decide whether you wanted to buy it or not. We would stay in the booth and play it over and over until they asked us to leave because we had no money to buy it anyway! Somehow, Bob Greene managed to always come up with enough money to buy a copy of *Down Beat*, which we devoured!

One day, on the way home from school, I stopped in the Sears and Roebuck store because they had a record department. I asked the young lady if she might have a record that had just been broken in two. She said no and that most of the time they were broken in small pieces, but if she found one, she would save it for me. I stopped in there every afternoon until one day she said she had one. It was a record by Jimmy Dorsey and his orchestra, and it was broken cleanly in two. On one side was the song "Deep Purple," and the other side was a vocal by Helen O'Connell. I didn't care about vocals at that time, I just wanted to hear the band play. I ran home, found some white adhesive tape, fitted the two pieces together, and taped along the cracks on the vocal side.

I had my own combination of radio and record player, so I put it on the turntable, and aside from being a little wobbly and two small clicks as it went around, it played beautifully! (Years later I told Jimmy that story. He asked if I still had it, he would love to see it.)

My aunt sent me up to the corner drugstore for some medicine one day, and in the side window was a large, full-size colored cutout of Glenn Miller advertising Chesterfield cigarettes. The Miller band had a fifteen-minute radio show every evening, that I never missed. I asked Mr. Schiller, the owner of the drugstore, what he would do with that advertisement when they were done with it. He said, "Probably throw it away." I said, "Please don't do that, please save it for me." About a month later, I noticed it was out of the window! Excited, I ran into the store. Mr. Schiller saw me, went into the back room, and came back with Glenn Miller. I took it home and nailed it up on my bedroom wall. It was my prized possession!

By now, I had started taking trumpet lessons. My teacher was a five-foot-one Italian guy (What else!) by the name of Bill Pupa. At one time, he had been with Paul Whiteman's orchestra.

I liked going to his apartment, once a week, for two dollars an hour, not only because he was a good teacher, but he talked to me a lot about the band business.

After about six months, he said one day, "Daryl, you're going to play the trumpet, but you need to decide in which direction you want to go. If you want to be a jazz player, you better be a good one because there are a lot of them out there. Or you might decide to become a first trumpet player. A good lead player makes more money and is always in demand. Start thinking about it." (Great advice!) He said that I should take any job that came along and play all kinds of music and that in the future I would come across that style of music and know what to do. (More good advice!)

I must admit I didn't practice my lessons as much as I should. My triple tonguing was adequate, but then again, I wasn't trying to get into the Pittsburgh Symphony! How I did practice was by stuffing a handkerchief in a cup mute and playing along with Jimmie Lunceford records, trying to build up my range. Bobby Hackett once told about an ad he put in the paper. The ad read, "B flat trumpet for sale, excellent condition upper register, never used." (But just listen to what he could do with the lower and middle register!)

I started playing in some local neighborhood bands. In those days, every neighborhood had a band. Sometimes we would play a church gig that paid five dollars for the whole band. We would use the money to buy new arrangements. Stock arrangements cost 75¢.

I got a job at a roadhouse called the New Penn owned by Lou Pssarella, an Italian. We worked from 8:00 until 3:00 a.m., playing dance music and two shows. We made $18.75 a week (nonunion) and a spaghetti dinner on Friday night!

About that time, a new student joined our music class. His name was Victor Klemeck. He came from Europe to get an American high school education. He was nineteen years old and already an accomplished musician. He played the violin, but he could also compose and arrange music for dance orchestras.

He said he knew of a booking agency that could book our high school dance band for the summer. We were all excited! Clyde Costly's parents wouldn't let him go with us, so I became the first trumpet player.

School was over on June 30, so on July 1, we all boarded a train and headed for Charleston, South Carolina. We were to play at a nightclub outside of Charleston called Berkeley's Jungle Gardens. To get there, we had to go to the Greyhound bus station, get on a bus, and have the driver drop us off near the nightclub. When we finished the job at twelve o'clock, we had to run back out to the highway to catch the twelve fifteen bus back to Charleston. What a joint this was. It was right next to an army base, and soldiers and sailors would get into fights every night. They also didn't want to hear a bunch of fifteen-year-old kids playing swing music, so we were fired by the second week.

The agency said they had three nights for us at the MacArthur Ballroom in Wrightsville Beach, North Carolina. Somehow we got there, I don't remember how, and played the three nights. All I remember about that was that it was the beginning of the war, and no lights were allowed along the beachfront at night in case there was an enemy submarine out there somewhere. Also, this was my introduction to alcohol!

One of the guys had a pint of orange-flavored gin. Boy! Talk about getting sick!

Victor Klemeck told us we were booked into the Princess Anne Hotel in Richmond, Virginia. We got there by bus and moved into some kind of boarding house.

Victor went to the hotel to tell them that we arrived and to find out when we would start.

He came back with the bad news! They only hired union bands, so we had never even been considered! We were stranded! We all had to call home for bus fare to get back to Pittsburgh.

Then one day I got a call to join a local society band (which we called Mickey Mouse bands), Tommy Carlan and his orchestra. He worked at least three or four nights a week, and I would have to join the musicians' union. I went to the union office to apply for a card. They said I had to audition, and some guy took me into another room. I had my trumpet with me, and he said, "Play something." I was very nervous, but I started to play "Over the Rainbow." After about eight bars, he said, "Okay, kid, you're in. Go to the office and pay your initiation fee." I was now an official member of Local 60 AF of M (American Federation of Musicians). The union scale for a three- or four-hour dance job was $7.50. Wow! Now I was making close to $25 a week and still going to school.

I now had some pocket money and could afford a new record once in a while. I played hooky from school every week to go downtown to the Stanley Theater where all the big bands played, and I would sit through all four shows.

As I sat there, I had this feeling that there was a wide chasm between me and the musicians on stage and that I was going to have to work very hard to get across that gap.

(I feel now that the musicians and what is passing for music are on the same level with their audience.)

I had just turned sixteen, so my father bought me a car that I desperately needed to be able to get to these jobs I was playing. It was a 1936 Ford for which he paid $400.

I was never really close with my father until years later. I know he loved me, he just had difficulty expressing it.

It was now my junior year in high school, and my school work really began to suffer. I had absolutely no interest in anything but the trumpet and playing music. Neither my aunt nor my uncle had much education, so they didn't realize that I should be bringing home a lot more homework.

I am ashamed to say that I stole a pack of blank report cards and changed all the grades so that they wouldn't find out I was failing. I was so afraid that if they did, they might take my horn away.

I continued to play with several local bands. The jobs usually went until twelve or one o'clock in the morning, and by the time I got home, it could be three or four. So when I got up in the morning to go to school, I would get in my car, drive to Highland Park, park under a tree, and go to sleep. (So much for higher education.)

CHAPTER FOUR

"Tweedin' Kirby Watson"

I had turned eighteen by now, still working with local bands and falling farther and farther behind in school.

We heard that there was a new band in town, Bob Astor and his orchestra, playing at the Chatterbox of the William Penn Hotel, and that they were looking for a trumpet player and a saxophone player. My friend Danny Small played tenor and baritone sax. We were asked to come down and sit in with the band at a tea dance, like an audition.

This was by far the best band I had played in by this time. They played special arrangements and really swinging music. I found out later that these arrangements had been given to Bob by black bandleaders like Lionel Hampton and Count Basie, mostly arrangements they didn't want anymore like "Tweedin' Kirby Watson!" (I never did find out what that meant). Bob Astor called his band a Lunceford sound with a Basie beat! We both passed the audition. The band was leaving town on Thanksgiving Day, and if we were going with them, we had to be in the hotel that day by twelve noon.

Now, how was I going to tell my aunt and uncle that I would not be graduating from high school, and that I wanted to go on the road with this orchestra.

I know they were very disappointed, but they knew how much I loved my music; and with the help of my trumpet teacher, I convinced them that it was pointless to force me to go back to school. (No bandleader ever asked me for a high school diploma!)

Danny and I showed up at noon with the rest of the band and waited around for the leader. Finally at four o' clock, one of the guys came and told us that Bob was upstairs in a poker game, gambling with the band payroll.

We were told to go to the train station and get ourselves to Youngstown, Ohio, check in to the Todd Hotel where we would be playing at the new Elm Ballroom.

The guy at the ticket window asked if we would like the parlor car. Youngstown was only sixty miles away, so Danny and I, being two naïve young kids, said, "Sure." The tickets were six dollars apiece!

The next day at the ballroom, Bob started paying the guys for their transportation. When he got to Danny and I, and we gave him our ticket stubs, he screamed, "What the hell is this? Twelve dollars? The parlor car?" I guess we looked so scared, he finally calmed down and paid us.

Our salary was supposed to be $50 a week, but as I remember, we didn't always get that full amount! (Bob liked to gamble!)

Bob Astor was a tall, six-foot-four good-looking guy. He wasn't a musician, didn't play an instrument, or read music, but he looked great in front of the band in his white dinner jacket. He was from New Orleans and was a drinking buddy of Charlie Barnet. He had his shirts tailor-made with widespread collars. I thought that was really hip! (Today that would mean cool!)

He smoked Parliament cigarettes at fifty cents a box. They had a hard paper tip that he could clench between his teeth as he talked. Naturally, I had to have Parliaments too. I smoked them for years.

We had very good musicians in the band. Dave Pell, age sixteen, a wonderful young saxophone player who went on a few years later to be featured with the Les Brown Orchestra and has recorded many albums with his own octet.

Bob Astor's band was what could be called a stepping-stone band: similar to Dean Hudson and Bob Chester, not the caliber of the Dorseys, Goodman, or James, but good bands where young musicians could get the experience and hopefully move up to that higher level. (Sorry to say, there is nothing like that anymore.)

We continued on the road, playing one-nighters until we were booked into the Vanity Ballroom outside of Detroit Michigan for three months, playing four nights a week.

Everything was going great. I had a crush on the girl singer, Mary Glover, also from Pittsburg, Kansas, that is! Nothing ever came of it, we were just good friends.

One day, I got a call from home saying that I had been notified by my draft board to appear for a physical on March 11.

I told Bob I had to leave, and he said, "Don't worry, they might not take you," (he himself was classified 4-F). "Your job will be here when you come back." He said, "If they do take you, make sure that when you fill out any forms asking about occupation, hobbies, or anything else, put down *musician*, every chance you get!"

I returned to Pittsburgh, passed the physical, and was inducted into the service on April 9, 1943!

CHAPTER FIVE

On the Boardwalk in Atlantic City

I guess I felt the same way as most of the young guys that showed up at the Pennsylvania Railroad Station that evening, ready to get on a train to go who knows where. Feeling patriotic and ready to go do our duty and get this thing over as soon as possible, thinking it shouldn't be long. (We were dreaming!)

We were herded into the train (No parlor car this time!). All the window shades in the coach were pulled down, with an MP at each end of the car to make sure they stayed that way. We were given a box lunch, which consisted of a sandwich, a banana, and a chocolate brownie. The train pulled out of the station, and we were on our way!

When the train stopped the next morning, we were all anxious to know where we were. We had stopped at a siding (no station platform) and loaded onto these large olive green trucks. After a short drive, we passed under a sign that said Welcome to Fort Meade. We were at the induction center of Fort Meade, Maryland.

We were marched up to a building that served as barracks, told to pick out a bunk, hustled outside, and told to line up. A sergeant marched us up to another building, took us inside a large room, and hollered, "Strip! Everything off, and line up!"

An officer with a clipboard, we assumed to be a doctor, walked behind the line, tapped each guy on the shoulder, and said, "Assume the position, [which meant bend over], and spread!"

Moving to the front of the line, he said, "Prepare for short-arm inspection!" If you haven't been in the army, you wouldn't know what that means, and I'm not going to describe it here!

About five o'clock, we were marched up to the mess hall. Inside was a large sign that said Take All You Want, Eat All You Take. As I remember, the food wasn't too bad, but then again, we were very hungry.

Back in the barracks about six, I had just settled down when a sergeant came in.

"The following men fall in outside." And he called up six names from a list, one of them mine.

We were taken back to the mess hall, around to the rear entrance; and once inside, a guy in white pants, a T-shirt, and white apron, pointed to me and another kid and gestured to follow him.

He took us to a large table on which were dozens of loaves of white bread, two huge jars—one filled with peanut butter, the other with jelly. "We need a thousand sandwiches by eleven o'clock for a troop train, so get busy!" (This was known as KP duty—kitchen police.)

It took us a little longer than eleven o'clock, but we finally finished.

I figured that was about it and that I could get back to bed until the guy in white came back and said, "Okay, follow me."

He led us to another area that was the bakery. He showed us the huge black ovens in which large pans of peach and cherry cobbler were being cooked.

He gave us a pair of heavy gloves and showed us how, after the timer goes off, to open the oven door, take these hot pans by the handles, and put them on a cooling table.

These pans were so hot that even through the gloves you could feel the heat! Not only that, but the cobbler was bubbling and oozing out of the crust. I was afraid of being scalded.

When they finished baking the cobbler, I thought to myself, *Thank God it's over!* But it wasn't. We were given large buckets of soap and water, a scrub brush and were told to scrub the floor. I thought to myself, *If this is the army, I hate it!*

It still wasn't over. After the floor dried, we had to polish it while a corporal stood over us to make sure we did it right.

It was now about 4:00 a.m., and our tormentor finally said, "Okay, you're through, you can go back to your barracks."

Still in my street clothes, I fell on my bunk and closed my eyes.

I was awakened by a shrill, piercing whistle and somebody hollering, "Drop your cocks and grab your socks!"

This was a nightmare!

We were lined up and marched to the mess hall for breakfast.

The rest of the morning was spent in processing and paperwork.

Remembering Bob Astor's advice, I wrote musician every chance I got.

The psychiatrists asked me if I liked girls and if I was a conscientious objector. When he was satisfied with my answers, he picked up a rubber stamp and stamped Air Corps on my papers and put them in the outbox.

After lunch, we were finally issued uniforms. Two sets of everything. Underwear, T-shirts, ODs (olive drabs), light khakis (suntans), fatigues, hats, caps, shoes (They even had my size-6!), leggings, helmet liner, and a large duffel bag. We had to put our civilian clothes away and wear the uniform from then on. We were told to be ready to ship out soon.

Once again, we were on a train bound for who knows where! The next morning, we pulled into a station where the sign read Atlantic City. I was to start my thirteen weeks of basic training, and I thought, *This shouldn't be too bad.*

After a short truck-ride, we stopped in front of a huge hotel, actually the Ambassador Hotel, and were assigned rooms. My room, shared with seven other guys, was on the twelfth floor; and we were told we could not use the elevators, only the stairs.

The Air Corps had taken over all the hotels in Atlantic City, stripped them down to bare walls and floors, put in double-decker bunks and footlockers. One bathroom for eight guys!

Our day started at 5:00 a.m., dress in fatigues, run down twelve flights of stairs to the mess hall, which had been the hotel ballroom, have one-half hour for breakfast then go outside and line up.

Most days, we would march two miles to the airport, which served as a drill field, and practice close-order drill, which meant learning to march in formation. Right face, left face, about-face, etc.

Back to the hotel about noon, lunch and maybe a half hour of free time to use the bathroom if you wanted to climb twelve flights of stairs!

After a couple of weeks, we were given a carbine rifle and taken to the range to learn how to use it. I qualified for sharpshooter and got a little silver medal to pin on my uniform.

Now that we had rifles, we had to practice extended-order drill, which meant doing all of our formations on the sandy beach in front of the hotel and also learning how to land on the beach from landing craft.

This was still April, and some days could be bitter cold, which made crawling around in wet sand miserable.

One weekend, my aunt and uncle came for a visit and brought my trumpet with them. My friend from high school Clyde Costly also wound up in Atlantic City, so some nights, if we didn't leave the hotel, we would play duets.

If we wanted to leave the hotel after dinner, we could get a pass, which was good until ten o'clock. Sometimes we would hike down to the Steel Pier; servicemen could get in free and listen to the house band they had led by Alex Bartha. We would stay until nine forty-five and then run up the boardwalk to get back to the hotel by ten. (Some years later, I would play the Atlantic City Steel Pier with four different bands: Tony Pastor, Charlie Spivak, Tommy Dorsey, and Richard Maltby Sr.)

One morning, around my twelfth week of basic training, we were lined up in formation in front of the hotel when our platoon sergeant called out my name. He told me to fall out and pack up my gear. I was being transferred out of Atlantic City. Later that morning, a truck picked me up, with three other guys in it, and headed for the train station. Once again, I was on my way to who knew where!

CHAPTER SIX

"Off We Go into the Wild Blue Yonder"

Seventeen of us got off the train at Pawling, New York, a small village about seventy-two miles from New York City. We discovered we were all musicians from different parts of the country.

After a short ride in a kind of school bus, we passed through a stone gate manned by MPs with rifles.

Up the driveway, we saw a large vine-covered building that looked like a college. We found out later that it had been a prep school for boys, but the government had taken it over and turned it into the Air Corps technical training school where they taught these bright new recruits cryptography, one of only two such schools, the other being in Colorado.

Cryptography was the art of sending and decoding secret messages. These students all had above-average intelligence and were sworn to secrecy.

They put us in a large dormitory, but many areas at the school were off-limits to us.

We were not an official Air Corps band, so we were attached to the MPs.

After a few days, they moved us out of the dormitory and into a large building off the main grounds. They called it the field house. It was originally used as an athletic compound for the prep school. It became our headquarters, which we liked because it separated us from the regimented atmosphere of the school, although we took all of our meals in their mess hall.

We had our own sleeping area, latrine facilities, and a large room we turned into a rehearsal hall.

The first rehearsal was spent practicing marches. The first one being the Air Corps song "Off We Go into the Wild Blue Yonder."

There was a large field in front of our building that had been used for football, soccer, and track events.

One of the trombone players, Glenn Heinlein, had been a drum major at Ohio State University (they made him a sergeant), so our mornings were spent out on the field, practicing marching band formations. One of our functions was to play for retreat every evening when all the students from the school would march down to the field to attend the ceremony. Quite often, the local townspeople would come to watch the proceedings.

In the afternoon, we would rehearse dance arrangements or concert-style arrangements of composers like George Gershwin. We all enjoyed these afternoons.

The countryside around Pawling was lovely; everything was lush and green and had the smell of freshly cut grass, but there wasn't much to do in the evening. Once or twice we took the train into New York City, went to places like the Metropole to hear Roy Eldridge or up to Fifty-second Street where we could get into the clubs for nothing and stand in the back to hear Art Tatum or the King Cole Trio.

Sometimes we would play a concert at the school or a dance at the local country club. We were there for about two months when suddenly the post was deactivated, and everyone was transferred out of Pawling. (Once again, a train ride to who knew where.)

And I certainly had no idea that where I was going would be the place where I would spend the next two and a half years of my life.

CHAPTER SEVEN

"If the Japs Only Knew What Our Arranging Staff Could Do!"

W e stepped off the train on a hot and muggy morning in Greensboro, North Carolina, piled into a large green truck and headed toward our destination, which was known as BTC Number 10. (BTC is short for Basic Training Center.) This was a real camp full of soldiers, barracks, and mud. We were put up in some temporary barracks right next to the WAC (Women's Army Corps) barracks and were ordered not to fraternize. We were told we were to be attached to the 724th and 725th Air Corps bands. There were about sixty musicians housed in two barracks. Bernie Privan, a fine trumpet player, who had been with several name bands, was there but soon after was sent up to New Haven to join the Glenn Miller band. A very young Med Flory, who later became an actor in Hollywood and also organized the Supersax, was there for a short time.

For at least two weeks, it seemed as though no one knew we were there. Our names were not read at roll call, and we were not assigned to any duties; so every morning, we would hang around behind the PX, drink 3.2 beer, and fuck off!

Up to this point, I hadn't been much of a drinker, and 3.2 beer didn't give you much of a buzz unless you drank a gallon of it. It was the only alcohol available, and as we found out later, the county we were in was dry! Eventually, they found us and assigned us to the concert band.

Within this organization, there were several groups. The concert band, the marching band, and the elite, which was known as the radio band led by a second lieutenant by the name of Harry Taylor. Apparently, Lieutenant Taylor was a favorite of the commanding general of the technical training command and so was given carte blanche where the radio band was concerned. They had eight brass, five saxophones, four legitimate reeds, two French horns, a full string section, and their own arranging and copying staff. It was called the radio band because they broadcasted from the camp every week and also participated in war bond drives. To justify having the string players, arrangers, and copyists, they had to march with the marching band playing the bass drum, glockenspiel, or some fake instrument and look as though they were playing. Taken from the radio band was a sixteen-piece dance band called the "A" band led by Warrant Officer Floyd Smith.

The camp was relatively new, so construction was still going on. After a few weeks, we were moved into a new area: two barracks as living quarters, a dayroom that also served as a rehearsal hall, a separate barrack for the arrangers and copyists, and one that served as administration and office for Lieutenant Taylor. The base was growing, and a new NCO (noncommissioned officer) club, a new officers club, and a posttheater were built. Lieutenant Taylor decided another dance band was needed, and it would be made up of musicians from the concert band and known as the B Band.

We had about eight trumpet players in the band, but only one besides myself that had any dance band experience. His name was Bob Baylis, and he had been with Ina Ray Hutton's orchestra before the war. He was a big friendly, easygoing guy who looked like Alan Hale. He was the lead trumpet player with the radio band and a pretty robust drinker. The guys in the concert band were asked to vote for someone to be the leader of the B Band, and I guess because I was the only one that had any dance band experience and could play lead trumpet, they picked me. We were given about twenty old stock arrangements and started to rehearse. I had some very good musicians with me: Moe Wexler on piano, Bob Zwally, a drummer that had been with me in Pawling, Cy Schatsberg on lead alto, and a good jazz tenor player, Barney Marino. I was now promoted to corporal—$66 a month instead of $53.

Sadly, I received a phone call from home that my dear uncle Jack had passed away. The Red Cross got me a three-day pass and supplied transportation money for me to go home for the funeral. My aunt received a small pension from the railroad, certainly not enough to live on, so I arranged for an allotment deducted from my pay, matched by the army, to be sent to her each month.

During this period of the 1940s, believe it or not, the army was segregated. The so-called colored section had their own band, and we were not to fraternize with them. Of course, we paid no attention to that; and sometimes at night, they would sneak down to our dayroom, or we would go up to theirs and sit around playing records, have a few drinks, and talk about jazz. There were several great players in that band, including eighteen-year-old James Moody, who, after the war, played with Dizzy Gillespie and who is recognized as one of the great tenor saxophone players in jazz. Also Linton Garner, brother of Errol Garner, played piano and wrote arrangements. Linton wrote several arrangements for my B Band that were a refreshing change from the stale old stock arrangements we had. We had one purpose in mind, to get as good or better than the A Band, and we were getting better! We played the officers club, the NCO Club, the USO Club in downtown Greensboro; and then we were given our own radio show *Parade Rest* from the posttheater once a week. Neither of the other trumpet players could play lead, so I had to sit with the section while Warrant Officer Smith conducted my band. We were becoming more popular with the enlisted men and the officers club than the A Band, which apparently didn't sit too well with the hierarchy!

One morning, I was summoned to Lieutenant Taylor's office. I saluted and stood at attention. He was very gracious and offered me a chair. "I heard your band the other night at the officers club and was very impressed. I like the way you play, reminds me of that trumpet player, ah, Henry Armstrong." (I figured he meant Louis Armstrong and didn't know the difference, but maybe I was wrong. After all, he was the lieutenant!) I said, "Thank you, sir." He continued, "How would you like to join the radio band?"

"Well, sir, I'm very happy with the B Band."

"I think you'll be happier with the radio band, Corporal."

I knew that what he asked was not a question, but an order! My B Band was given to Sergeant Fred Lambert, the trumpet player I replaced in the radio band. Freddie was a good guy but a lot more military than me, and the guys in the B Band weren't too happy. As I look back now, Lieutenant Taylor did me a big favor because the experience I got playing with a studio-type orchestra was invaluable. Also, when the war took a turn for the worse because of the Battle of the Bulge, many musicians were taken out of the bands and sent overseas to be stretcher bearers. No one in the radio band was touched because we were valuable to the war bond drives we did.

My new companions became Bob Baylis, Bob Pring, the lead trombone player in the radio band, and Irving Frank, the lead alto player.

One evening, the four of us were hanging out in the dayroom, listening to records and drinking Coke spiked with cheap rum from a bottle that Baylis had brought with him. Someone came up with the bright idea to attach animal names to guys that resembled them. For instance, Bob Baylis with his mane of blond curly hair looked like a lion. Bob Pring was a colt, Irv Frank was a crab, George Faber was a fawn because of his soft doelike eyes. I only weighed about 110 pounds and displayed some nervous energy on occasion, so Bob Pring said, "You're the flea!" That's how it happened, and it stuck! We had several others, but time has dimmed the memory. How the title for this chapter came about was because of two of the funniest guys I ever knew. Harry Doran and Mickey Steinke composed "If the Japs Only Knew What Our Arranging Staff Could Do." Harry played guitar, and Mickey was a good Dixieland-style drummer. They were also bunkmates and notable drinkers! One morning during an inspection, they told Mickey to open his footlocker. He lifted the lid; and in the top tray were his socks, underwear, belts, etc., neatly folded and lined up in order. The officer lifted out the top tray, and there in the center of the bottom of the footlocker was a small American flag. Both Doran and Steinke snapped to attention and saluted! It was hilarious! Hanging out with Bob Baylis required imbibing more than I had before, and I guess it was because I wanted to be accepted by someone I looked up to. Liquor was not easy to come by in Greensboro unless you went to a bootlegger and paid top dollar. I discovered that if I hitchhiked to Danville, Virginia, about fifty miles away, I could buy liquor at the state store. A bottle of Old Rocking Chair, aged three months, could be had for about three dollars. For a little over fifteen bucks, I could bring back five bottles, keep two for myself, and sell the other three at the officers club for at least $10 apiece! I made that trip once about every ten days. I also discovered White Lightning, homemade corn liquor we got from a bootlegger, at five bucks a gallon. If you cut it with grape juice, it was more palatable. That was known as a purple Jesus! It sure was a different kind of high, and I really liked it.

One night, we were to play a concert at the USO. I don't remember who, but somebody handed me a Coke and a white pill marked with an X. "Here, this'll give you a good kick." We were in the middle of a concert band arrangement of Stravinsky's Firebird suite when it hit! What a feeling! All my senses became sharpened, the sound was magnified, and I felt as though I were sitting in the middle of the New York Philharmonic! I also didn't sleep for the next two days. I found out later it was Benzedrine. In those days, you could go to a drugstore, buy a Benzedrine inhaler, break it apart, tear the paper that was saturated with Benzedrine into strips, soak it in 3.2 beer, and stay high for days. (Of course, the comedown was another story.)

Just before the holidays, I was invited to a Christmas party. I didn't want to go because I didn't know anyone there, but whoever invited me said there was free booze! I was standing off in a corner by myself, feeling out of place, when a cute young girl walked up to me and said, "Hey, my name is Midge, would you like a drink?" and handed me a glass of Southern Comfort over crushed ice. Nat King Cole's record of the "The Christmas Song" was playing in the background. I fell hard right then and there! We spent the rest of the evening talking and getting to know each other. She lived in High Point, North Carolina, just fifteen miles from Greensboro and worked at the base as a secretary to one of the officers. Most of the Southern girls I had met up until then seemed shallow and artificial. Midge was different; she was independent and understood how I felt about my music. The universe had provided the perfect scenario! Holiday atmosphere, lonely soldier, pleasant drink, Nat King Cole in the background, and a pretty girl. Thus began a two-year love affair.

Bob Pring also met a nice girl, Jean Atkinson, who was a very good singer. Jean had a sister, Betty, who I had dated once or twice. We both liked music and art, but that was about the extent of it. Just good friends. Our friend Irv Frank began seeing Betty, so the six of us triple dated. Pring wound up marrying Jean, and not long after, Irv married Betty. (I am very sorry to say that Bob Pring and I are the only ones alive today.)

There was a contingent at the base called special services. One of their duties was to put on variety shows and radio shows with skits patterned around army life. They had a group of actors, one I remembered distinctly, a young Pfc (private first class) by the name of Charlton Heston who was not very good at reading his lines.

BTC Number 10 had been changed to an ORD (Overseas Replacement Depot) where men were sent overseas or returned from overseas. One of our duties was to play for the troop trains coming and going. Special services began bringing in performers to entertain these troops. Donald O'Connor was there for about a month, and he hung around the band a lot. He was a nice, down-to-earth guy, and we became friends and spent some time together. (We met again years later while I was working at Disney World in Orlando, Florida.) The singer Tony Martin did a couple of war bond tours with us. (I worked with him at the Copacabana in New York after the war.) While at the Copa, Tony told the guys in the band that if they wanted a good discount on a new "after six" tuxedo that he was endorsing, we should go downtown to a certain tailor and mention his name. The tailor said (with a Jewish accent), "If you vant a discount, tell Tony Martin to give it to you!"

Being in the radio band also meant that I would now be in the A Band. Bob Baylis was the first trumpet player, so I took over the second or jazz or chair. This gave me a chance to display my range that I had worked on, practicing with the Lunceford records. I thought it was hip to play the last note of an arrangement a third higher than the lead or to show off playing a certain passage an octave higher. (Ah, youth!) Now, if I'm playing lead in a band, and that happens when it isn't written or necessary, it bugs the shit out of me! They built a new ORD officers club, and the A Band would play there a couple of nights a week. They also started bringing in bands that might be traveling through our area and giving them a Monday night at the club. Bands like Dean Hudson, Bob Chester, and Guy Lombardo.

By 1945, the war had started to wind down, and when it was finally over, we all anxiously began to look forward to being discharged. Baylis, Pring, Irv Frank, and I were notified that we would be discharged by February 1946.

One Monday night in early January, the Tony Pastor band played at the officers club. The following night, the A Band played there. The Pastor band had the night off, so Tony and his manager, Charlie Trotta, were seated at a table near the bandstand listening to us. After the second set, our leader, Warrant Officer Smith, sat at Tony's table during the intermission. Just before we were to get back on the bandstand, he took Baylis, Pring, and I aside and told us Tony's manager wanted to talk to us when we were finished. After putting our horns away, we went over to the table, met Tony and his manager, and were invited to sit down. Charlie Trotta asked if we knew when we were to be discharged. We told him sometime in February. He said Tony wanted to make some changes in the band, and would the three of us be interested in joining them in Chicago.

Of course, we would! We shook hands, and Charlie Trotta said we would be hearing from them soon with the details. When their office called, they offered me $115 a week to play fourth trumpet and that I was to join the band in Chicago at the Panther Room of the Sherman Hotel in early March. I was ecstatic!

That great day finally came, February 4, when I became a civilian again, thirty-four months after that first train ride to Fort Meade. During the separation process, as we were packing up all our uniforms and equipment, a sergeant asked me what would I like to take home with me and that "fatigues were great for washing the car." I handed him my barracks bag and said, "Keep all of it," and walked away. Two weeks before my discharge, I bought a new suit—a one-button roll, a white shirt, a new tie, and shoes; I reserved a room at the O. Henry Hotel and had five bottles of whiskey for my friends and I to celebrate. Two days later (with a hangover), I was on a train bound for Pittsburgh and the future!

CHAPTER EIGHT

"All That Glitters Is Not Gold"

After a few weeks at home, I took my first plane flight to Chicago. Baylis, Pring, and I were told to meet, check in to the Croydon Hotel, come down to the Panther Room that evening, and sit at the bar. We would join the band the next night. I couldn't believe I was actually there. I certainly had heard about the Panther Room because a lot of the name bands played there. Tony's band sounded great! Seven brass, five saxophones, four rhythms, male and female singers, and a vocal group. Charlie Trotta found us and said, "Tomorrow night, be here an hour before we start to get your jackets and take a look at the book." The three of us went back to the Croydon and stopped at the bar. It was called the Circle bar because it was round with a piano player on a platform in the center. It was also open twenty-four hours a day. (During the next few years, I spent many nights there.) I finally went up to my room, opened the door, and met my new roommate. His name was Tommy Lynn (Leonetti), the seventeen-year-old male vocalist with Tony's band. The vocal group called the Tunetimers was made up of Tommy and his four sisters. (They all had the same Italian nose!) We hit it off right away, became good friends, and, a few years later, worked together again with the Charlie Spivak Orchestra. Tony's girl singer was Virginia Maxey, a petite blonde with a good voice.

I have to pause for a moment to relate this story. About three nights after I had joined the band, I went back to the hotel after work, stopped for a drink, and went up to our room. I got in bed, turned out the light, and prepared to go to sleep. A few minutes later, I heard a key in the lock opening the door, and in comes Tommy with a girl. I heard her whisper,

"Oh! There's somebody in here." Tommy said, "Don't worry, that's my roommate, he's asleep."

"Are you sure?"

"Yeah, don't worry." I had my eyes closed, but I could hear everything. He got her into bed, and after a few minutes of silence. "Tommy, sing something for me." He started to croon "That Old Feeling." I tried not to giggle by stuffing the pillow in my mouth, but I couldn't control it.

"He's awake! He's awake!"

"No, no, no, I'm sure he's not, it'll be okay!" "I gotta go, I gotta go!" Poor Tommy, he struck out.

Bobby Geyer played first trumpet with Tony's band. Stubby Pastor, Tony's brother, played second, Baylis was on the split-lead chair, and I played fourth. Bob Pring was given the second trombone chair.

Geyer didn't seem too friendly, but we had heard that he and the two trumpet players Baylis and I had replaced were close friends. He was bugged about them having been fired. The arrangements weren't very difficult, so I was having fun sight-reading. I noticed as I read the arrangements that if the next passage on the part noted straight mute, Geyer would pick up a cup mute. I assumed he knew best, so I put a cup mute in the bell of my horn. Suddenly he put down the cup mute and picked up a straight mute, leaving Baylis and I hanging with the wrong mute in our horn. He did this several times. At the first intermission, I asked Stubby what was going on. He said, "Don't pay any attention to him, he's probably drunk, just use the mute the arrangement calls for." I never did get to know Bobby Geyer well because he quit and was gone two weeks later. It was great being in Chicago, especially for a twenty-one-year-old kid who had just spent two and a half years in the service. Playing with a name band, earning $460 a month instead of $66, hanging out in musician bars like the Croydon Circle, Davey Millers, and the Warm Friends Tavern. The after-hours clubs where we would play a dice game called twenty-six for free drinks, and after, the girls that ran the game who got to know us would let us win. Wonderful restaurants like the Corner House, the Singapore for Chinese ribs, or the Corona steakhouse where if you went in the rear entrance and sat at the counter, you could have a good steak for two dollars. If you went through the front door and sat at a table, the same steak was for four dollars!

A new lead player was brought in, Dominic Geracie, from Chicago. He was a fine player. The first note for lead trumpet on Tony's theme song "Blossoms" was an A flat above the staff, which could be a bastard note for trumpet, easy to miss. I don't think I ever heard Dominic miss it!

One night at the end of the week, Charlie Trotta made an announcement that the following night the band would have a recording session after work. Wow! How exciting! I would be playing on a real record.

The next night, after work, we walked to the recording studio as it was just a few blocks from the Sherman Hotel. The trumpet section was on a riser with four black metal music stands. The new arrangements had been passed out and put on the stands. They were written by Ralph Flanagan, who later went on to have his own successful band. The session was scheduled for three hours. (In 1946, a three-hour session paid $33.50.) The first side we recorded was a tune called "Sioux City Sioux" featuring Tony on the vocal.

Kind of a silly song. "Sioux City Sioux, Sioux City Sioux, her hair is red, her eyes are blue, I'd swap my horse and dog for you."

After a short break, we came back to record the second side. Bob Baylis said, "Let's switch parts, you do this one." It was a rhumba called "All That Glitters Is Not Gold." The introduction featured a trumpet solo in a straight mute, Latin style. Before I had a chance to give the part back to Bob, Tony beat it off. I played it using a fluttertongue style that I had heard Latin trumpet players use. Tony looked up, surprised, but didn't say anything. We rehearsed it a couple of more times and then did the final take. I think that when Baylis saw the solo, he got nervous; I didn't have enough time to get nervous! (Also, I had had a few drinks before the session and wasn't feeling any pain!)

We finished the engagement at the Sherman and set out on a tour of one-nighters headed toward the East Coast. Tony leased a large bus from American Orchestra, a company that supplied transportation for several name bands. With Tony, sixteen guys in the band, six singers, Tony's manager, Charlie Trotta, and Dan Gregory, the road manager, most seats were taken. Bob Pring and I grabbed two seats in the back so that we could nip on our jugs during the one-nighters. A few of the guys in the band were married and were allowed to bring their wives on the bus. Not good! Constant bickering and jealousy were rampant. (Of all the bands I played in, this was the only one where wives were allowed to travel with us on the bus.)

We got to New York and were booked into the Café Rogue at the Hotel Pennsylvania for a three-week engagement. I checked in to the President Hotel on Forty-eighth Street between Broadway and Eighth Avenue where most of the traveling bands stayed when in New York. A double room was seven dollars plus $0.21 tax. I also was introduced to Charlie's Tavern, a warm, friendly bar that catered to musicians. The local musicians hung out there plus most of the guys with the road bands that came through town. Charlie's became like a second home. It was owned by Charlie English, a robust balding man, who was an easy touch for musicians down on their luck. I doubt whether Charlie ever recovered all of the money he was owed. The bar stayed open until 4:00 a.m., and if you wanted a bottle to take back to your hotel, Charlie would give it to you as long as you replaced it the next day.

There was a bar, Kelly's, across the street from the side entrance of the Hotel Pennsylvania where we would go for a quick drink between sets. One night in Kelly's, standing at the bar, I heard the first few bars of Tony's theme coming from the radio. I had forgotten we were doing a broadcast from the Café Rogue. I rushed back to the hotel through the kitchen into the Café Rogue and jumped up on the bandstand. The band had a policy about being late for anything. It meant a fine of $18.75 deducted from your pay at the end of the week for any infraction. A treasury bond was purchased with the money, and at the end of the month, a drawing was held in which you draw for any bond except for the one or more, on some occasions, you were responsible for.

During the second week of our New York engagement, I called my girlfriend in Greensboro and invited her to join me for the weekend. I reserved a room at a modest hotel two blocks from the Café Rogue so as to save her any embarrassment. (Things were different in those days.) We were having a good time, sightseeing, making love, and just being together. I was drinking quite a bit, and every time I got loaded, I proposed. She would just laugh and say, "Have another drink."

That Saturday morning, Tony's band was to be featured on Johnny Desmond's *Teentimers* radio show. On Friday night, Midge and I didn't get back to our hotel until 5:00 a.m. Needless to say, I did not wake up on Saturday morning and missed the broadcast completely! This did not endear me with Tony's manager. Plus another $18.75!

One night, near the end of the Café Rogue engagement, Tony and his brother Stubby got into an argument on the bandstand. Tony made a remark about Stubby's trumpet solo, and Stubby yelled something back. We finished the set and were leaving the bandstand with Tony and Stubby still hollering at each other. A group of people were standing in front of the bandstand, waiting to talk to Tony and get an autograph. Stubby came down from the trumpet section and continued to argue. Tony said, "If I didn't have a band you wouldn't have a job!" Stubby answered, "If Uncle Louis hadn't financed you, you wouldn't have a band." It got a little physical, no fisticuffs for fear of hitting each other in the mouth, but they began to kick each other in the shins. Quite a funny scene!

Bob Baylis lived on Long Island, so he decided to give his notice, get off the road, and stay home. Bob Pring received an offer from Tex Beneke to take over the first trombone chair, so he also quit the band. I think Virginia Maxey also left about that time. (She later married Matt Dennis, a fine piano player/composer.)

When Baylis gave his notice, I asked Charlie Trotta for a chance to move over to the relief lead chair. He fluffed me off and said he had already hired another trumpet player from Chicago. A friend of Dominic Geracie, Corny Panico. I understood and said no more about it. Corny was a nice guy, and we hung out together a lot. He was a decent player but wasn't cut out to play lead.

We left New York and headed for our next engagement. The Steel Pier in Atlantic City.

Two new singers joined the band. They were sisters from a small town in Kentucky, across the river from Cincinnati, Ohio, Rosemary and Betty Clooney. Rosemary was seventeen and Betty was fifteen. Their uncle Nick traveled with them as a chaperone. Tony had Ralph Flannagan write some new arrangements for them. They were very sweet girls, and the guys in the band liked them, although Uncle Nick kept them at a distance. No need to tell you about Rosemary Clooney. She went on to be one of the top stars on records, television, and movies. The girls and I became good friends, and I had the pleasure of working with Rosie quite often in the ensuing years.

We were scheduled to record an album of Disney songs from the movie *Song of the South,* and one evening, I heard Tony and Charlie Trotta discussing the situation about Corny and the fact that he wasn't really making it on the split lead chair. Tony probably hadn't said ten words to me since I joined the band, so I took a gamble and said to him, "Tony, I would like a chance in that chair, I know I can do it." I could see Charlie Trotta fuming! He started to say something, but Tony said, "Okay, Flea, we'll give it a try." I knew right then that I had made an enemy of Charlie Trotta! Corny and I switched places, and things seemed to be going fine. Actually, Corny was relieved. It took the pressure off him.

One day, about a month or so later, I was a minute or two late getting on the bus, and I refused to allow them to take the $18.75 fine out of my paycheck. When payday came, Dan Gregory, the road manager, gave me my check and my two weeks' notice! Charlie Trotta considered me to be a rebel and had found a reason to let me go. If I had known then what I know now, I certainly would have handled that whole situation differently; but as they say, live and learn. (Ironically, I heard a few years later that Charlie Trotta committed suicide by jumping out of a window.)

I didn't want to face going home, having been fired, so I decided to visit my friend Bob Baylis who lived in Patchogue, Long Island.

I rode the Long Island Railroad train to Patchogue. Bob picked me up at the station and proceeded to show me all the local bars he frequented. About the third night, we had been drinking all day, and at 3:00 a.m., he said, "I know where we can find a horse, so let's go for a ride." We got in his car, and after a short drive, we found this pasture with an old swayback horse standing there asleep. We climbed over the fence, both of us smashed, and staggered over to this magnificent steed. Baylis tried to climb on his back but couldn't make it. I said, "Give me a boost, I'll show you how to do it!" I got on his back, gave him a little kick, and said, "Giddyup." The horse turned his head, looked at me, reared up on his hind legs, tossing my "ass over tin cup" off his back and onto the ground then took off down the pasture. I landed hard, and when I tried to get up, the pain almost made me pass out. Baylis carried me to the car as I couldn't walk. He drove us back to his place and put me on the couch. For the next two days, we continue drinking, in my case, to dull the pain. I had gone through what was left of my last paycheck, so I called home and asked my aunt to send me train fare back to Pittsburgh. To this day, I can still feel the spot where I landed that night. A chiropractor told me that if I hadn't started treatment when I did, I would be limping by the age of thirty. (I never saw Baylis again. He passed away in a mental institution some years later.)

CHAPTER NINE

The Peppy Pirates/
"Open the Door, Richard"

Back in Pittsburgh, in the fall of 1946, I began playing with some local bands again. One in particular I really enjoyed. Brad Hunt's orchestra. It was a good band with five brass, four saxophones, and two vocalists. The band worked an average of three nights a week and sometimes a local location job. All the arrangements were written by Al Powell, one of the trumpet players. Al was influenced by the Jimmie Lunceford Orchestra, and that style crept into many of the arrangements he wrote. I had grown up listening to the Lunceford band, so Al and I hit it off immediately. We became very close friends and drinking buddies. Many nights, I would drive to his house, either he had a bottle or I would bring one, and spend hour after hour listening to records and sharing the love we had for music.

Early in 1947, I got a call from Baron Elliott who had the staff orchestra on radio station WCAE. Originally, he had a Lombardo-style band, very corny; but the staff band consisted of six brass, five saxophones, four rhythms, and two vocalists. Baron himself played the soprano saxophone, kind of syrupy, but he was the leader. I joined the band on second trumpet, and my old friend from high school Clyde Costly was playing third. After a few months, Stan Cebek who played lead was let go, and I took over the first chair.

In 1947, Pittsburgh had four radio stations with staff orchestras. KDKA had Maurice Spitalny, brother of Phil Spitalny, with a large studio orchestra and a weekly program for Iron City Beer. Baron Elliott on WCAE, Lee

Kelton with the twelve-piece band on WJAS, and a quartet led by Joe Negri on KQV.

We did a fifteen-minute broadcast at 6:15 p.m., Monday through Friday, called the Stardust Melodies of Baron Elliott, and a one-hour show on Saturday. This paid $95 a week. Because of the exposure on radio, the band was very popular, so we played many single engagements around the Pittsburgh area. Once in a while, we would do a week at Bill Green's Casino for an additional $95. Boy! $190 a week was tops for a musician in Pittsburgh.

One day, Baron decided that we needed more variety on the Saturday broadcast, so aside from playing our instruments, we would become a glee club singing a cappella. The first song we did was "The Whiffenpoof Song." (Actually not too bad!)

Pittsburgh's baseball team was, and still is, the Pittsburgh Pirates. A contest was held to come up with a song for the team. The winner was "The Peppy Pirates" and was to be featured on our radio show. Baron decided that the glee club should sing it.

> *The Pirate crew is peppy, and a peppy crew are they,*
> *The pirate crew is peppy, and surely they'll win today,*
> *Just hear their bats a-crackin' with the Hip, Hip, Hooray!*
> *The pirate crew is peppy, and surely they'll win today*!

I hate to think of how the losers sounded!

We had some excellent musicians in Baron's band. One in particular, Sammy Nestico. Anyone in the music business would now know that name. He has become one of the premier arrangers, orchestrators, and all-around fine musicians on the jazz scene today!

When I first met Sammy, he was playing trombone with Baron's band. Not many people know what a fine trombone player he was. Let me give you an example.

When I was with the Tommy Dorsey Orchestra, and we were to play a one-nighter in Washington DC, our lead trombone player, Tak Tavorian, became ill and couldn't make the job. At that time, Sammy was in the service, stationed in Washington. I recommended him for the job. Tommy's road manager, Tino Barzie, called Sammy and asked if he could help us out for a few days. Sammy was excited! He had grown up as I had, listening and admiring Tommy Dorsey.

About the second night, Tommy got off the stand about midway during the second set. Lee Castle took over and called for a fake medley. Lee pointed to Sammy and said, "Play one." Sam said, "Okay." and called out to the piano player, "East of the Sun."

He was playing it beautifully when suddenly Tommy returned to the bandstand. Sammy finished and sat down. Tommy didn't say a word, called up the next tune, and continued the set. The next night, however, during a medley, Tommy looked at Sam and said, "Hey, kid, play 'East of the Sun.'" I know Sammy was nervous, but he went right at it. Tommy was smiling through the whole chorus. He said to Sammy that night, "Listen, kid, anytime you want to get out of the service, you have a job right here!" More about Sammy Nestico later.

The radio-station gig lasted through 1947 and into early 1948. One day, after our broadcast, Baron gave us the news that WCAE was canceling the Stardust Melodies program. This was the beginning of what was to become a national trend.

(Television was here and was fast becoming an entertainment media. People could watch it rather than just listen to it. The era of staff orchestras gradually came to an end, and as of now, there isn't one staff orchestra in this country, either on radio or television. Oh yes, a few late-night talk shows have small groups, but those are independent shows.)

Baron continued to book local jobs but not as many as before. I needed a salary, so when I got a call from Luke Reilly, the leader of the pit band at the casino burlesque theater, I grabbed it! It turned out to be probably the most fun I would ever have in the music business.

The band consisted of two trumpets, one trombone, one saxophone, bass, drums, and piano. (Five out of seven were drunkards!) We did four shows a day from 11:00 a.m. to 11:00 p.m., six days a week. Because of Pennsylvania's blue laws, live shows were not allowed to operate on Sunday, so we would come in on Sunday night and rehearse the new show for the following week from 10:00 p.m. to midnight. At 12:05 a.m., Monday morning, we would play one show then come back at 11:00 a.m. and start the new week. All this for $93 a week!

Luke Reilly was the leader and played piano. Kloman Schmidt played second trumpet, Elmer "Bunny" Droun played tenor saxophone, Red French was the drummer, Freddy Whitlinger handled the bass. I don't remember the trombone player's name. (He didn't drink!)

The so-called band room was under the stage with an entrance into the pit where you had to stoop down, work your way behind the piano and into your seat. Extra-added attraction! The chorus girls had to come down the stairs and walk right past the band room to go to the showers!

Each of us had a locker in which to keep our instruments and stash a jug. We had a large watercooler that held a five-gallon bottle of water on top, but we replaced it with a five-gallon jug of wine. Once a week, somebody had to scrape the wine flies off the drain plate. Between shows, we would go down the street to the Wheel Cafe, a friendly neighborhood bar, where the drinks were cheap and a free buffet lunch was available. Most of the burlesque people hung out there.

A lot of people have the mistaken impression that burlesque was dirty. Not true! Sure, the girls wore scanty costumes but never undressed all the way, leaving just enough to your imagination.

The comedians never used foul language. In place of Jesus Christ, they said "cheese and crackers!" Dirty bastard came out "dirty basket." I loved the comedians. Each week, one of the guys in the band had to stay in the pit during the comedy routines while the rest of the guys could get out of the pit to have another drink. At a certain phase in the routine, whoever was in the pit would push a buzzer to alert the rest of the band to get back in the pit. I volunteered many times to stay there because no matter how many times I heard their routines, I enjoyed listening to that kind of humor. Comedians like Pigmeat Markham, Moms Mabley, "Cheese and Crackers" Hagan, and Dusty Fletcher, who wrote "Open the Door, Richard."

I must tell you about New Year's Eve. On New Year's Eve day, we played our regular four shows and then played a midnight show then another show, which was called the milkman's matinee at 5:00 a.m. The audience was comprised of drunks and perverts. Needless to say that by 5:00 a.m., virtually every one in the show was bombed! During a production number of the song "Japanese Sandman," the chorus girls carried a pair of Japanese lanterns on their shoulders. Because they were loaded, some of them turned the wrong way and got the lanterns all tangled up! Resulting in total chaos! Another time when they were dancing in a line Rockettes style and doing the high kicks, some of the rubber falsies would fly out and bounce all over the stage and into the pit. Luke Reilly somehow finished the show then passed out with his head on the keyboard. Kloman Schmidt was so drunk he couldn't get out of his chair, so we just left him there, sound asleep until our first regular show at 11:00 a.m. on New Year's Day.

A few of the guys in the band dated some of the chorus girls. A short blonde, Marie, and I occasionally had a drink together at the Wheel Café. (She could match me drink for drink!) Soon, a close relationship developed. Not love, no commitment. Marie had a small room at a local hotel, not a four-star, not even a two-star, with a bathroom down the hall. Sometimes, because we worked all day and were together at night, I might not go home for two or three days. I still lived with my aunt, and this, no doubt, annoyed her. Her comment was, "I guess he's with that high kicker again!" I was supporting the household, so I assumed I could do as I pleased. The burlesque job lasted through 1948 and into early 1949.

The Pittsburgh musicians union had its own club with a bar and a small kitchen where you could get a huge plate of spaghetti for $0.75. Being a private club, it was open after hours.

One night, after finishing four shows, I was having a drink at the bar with my friend Al Powell. He told me that bandleader Charlie Spivak was sitting at one of the tables. His band was working at Bill Green's, a club out of town that I had played with Baron Elliott, and that Charlie was looking for a first trumpet player. Before I knew it, Al left the bar and went over to Spivak's table. After a few minutes, he motioned for me to come over. Apparently, he had been telling Spivak that I was what he was looking for. Charlie was very cordial and asked if I could come out to Green's some night after work and sit in with his band; they played until 1:00 a.m. The next night, Al picked me up at the theater, and we drove out to Bill Green's together.

The band was on a break, so Charlie's manager, Charlie Russo, said, "Get your horn out and sit in on the next set."

I was very comfortable sitting in the brass section. My chops were in good shape, and the band sounded wonderful. We finished the set, and Russo asked me if I would finish the night. I was having a good time, so I said, "Sure." We got back on the stand, and Russo and Charlie were in a huddle discussing something. Spivak said, "Get up. I Found Gold." I didn't know it at the time, but this was a great Neil Hefti arrangement that the band didn't play very often because the first trumpet part was rather demanding. After I finished the night, Spivak thanked me and said Russo would talk to me. Russo asked if I could be available sometime soon; he couldn't make a commitment now, but he would stay in touch. I was a little disappointed because I thought I had done well that night, but it wasn't up to me now.

One day, about three weeks later, we had just finished our first show when someone told me I had a long-distance phone call at the box office. It was Charlie Russo wanting to know if I could join Spivak's band the next week in Youngstown, Ohio. I took his number and said I would call him back. Even though it was only a one-week notice, Luke Reilly gave me his blessing and wished me luck. I called Russo and said I could be there. He said the first chair paid $135 a week and that I should come directly to the theater in Youngstown where the band was playing for three days, for a 10:00 a.m. rehearsal the following Monday.

Within a year, the Casino Theater had closed and along with the Wheel Café, would be torn down soon after. How sad! How sad!

CHAPTER TEN

"Stardreams" and "In Flew the Flea"

Charlie Spivak's band had six brass, three trumpets, and three trombones. Buddy Yannon (Ianonne), a fine melodic jazz player was on second; and Russ Motcalm, a solid section player, played third trumpet. All of the first trumpet parts were in my book except on occasion when Charlie would come back and play lead over the section.

Charlie was a wonderful trumpet player. He wasn't a jazz player, didn't swing, but no one could play a ballad more beautifully than he could. He was billed as "The Man Who Plays the Sweetest Trumpet in the World." (*When* asked if that were true, I always say, "Gee, I don't know. I never tasted it!" (Yuk, yuk) We finished the three-day theater in Youngstown and hit the road for a slew of one-nighters. In those days, one-nighters consisted mainly of ballrooms, one-day or three-day theaters, and an occasional one- or two-week location in theaters in the larger cities such as the Earle Theatre in Philadelphia, the State Theatre in Hartford, Connecticut, the Chicago Theater in Chicago, the Capitol, Paramount, or Loews State Theatre in New York. You could spend a month playing a chain of ballrooms in New England or the Midwest. (We once did ninety one-nighters in the state of Texas alone!) None of that exists today. Charlie's bus was leased by the Flying Eagle bus line out of Danbury, Connecticut. It had no air-conditioning, and the heater only worked half the time. Besides Charlie and the guys in the band, we had Irene Daye, the girl singer; Tommy Lynn, my friend from the Tony Pastor band; Charlie's valet; and Irene's maid. Some space in the back was set aside to hang Irene's gowns, and a large wooden case that held six pairs of Charlie's elevator shoes. (He wasn't very tall.)

At one of the theaters, the stage manager said that the band platform was brand-new, and he wouldn't allow Bobby Ricky, our drummer, to put spurs on his bass drum. (The spurs prevented the drum from moving forward but could dig into the floor because of the action of the bass drum pedal.)

Bobby had a great idea! He found some rope, tied it to the bass drum, ran it under the back curtain, and tied it to a radiator on the back wall of the theater. Everything went fine during rehearsal.

At the first show, Charlie gave the downbeat, and as the curtain opened, we went into the theme "Stardreams." What we didn't know was that the bandstand was on a hydraulic track. It started to slowly move toward the front of the stage. The slack went out of Bobby's ropes and began pulling the drum set off the back of the platform! Bobby was hollering, "Stop! Stop!" Thankfully, the stagehand saw what was happening and pushed the stop button. We finished the show to a seated ovation!

The guys in Charlie's band got along very well together, probably because Charlie was the most affable, easygoing bandleader. I never saw him fire anyone. For instance, we had a second trombone player, Russ Sonju, who looked like a character out of a Virgil Partch cartoon. Russ was a very heavy drinker, and at times, this sour, alcoholic smell would waft from the bell of his horn. Charlie, having to stand next to the trombone section at times, couldn't stand it. He told Russo to move Russ down two seats to the third chair. (Russ thought it was because Charlie felt he played better low notes.)

In those days, there were no interstate highways or thruways. If we had a four-hundred-mile trip that took all day and didn't have enough time to check in to a hotel before the job, Charlie would walk around, before we started, and tuck a $10 bill into the breast pocket of each guy in the band—$10 meant a lot then!

I don't remember how it happened, but somehow, my trumpet got bent and wouldn't play right. Charlie always carried at least three trumpets of his own made by Vincent Bach, so he told me to choose one and use it until I could get mine fixed. I found one I liked and played it for a couple of weeks. Charlie said he thought I sounded better on that horn than my own. I agreed and asked if he would be willing to sell it to me. We agreed on a price, and Charlie said he would take $10 a week out of my salary until it was paid. He did that for four weeks and then stopped. When I asked why, he said, "Forget it! I want you to have it." I worked for Charlie about two and a half years and during that time received two raises that I didn't even ask for. Granted they were small, one for five dollars and one for $10, but he was the only leader that ever did that.

I have another Tommy Lynn story to relate. As I said earlier, Tommy had a rather large nose. So during a week off, he decided to get a nose job. When we left New York to go back on the road, Tommy had this clamp he had to put on his nose to keep the bone straight while it healed. It had a small screw on the side so that he could tighten it just enough to keep it secure. One day on the bus, he fell asleep in his seat with the clamp in place. Bobby Ricky crept down the aisle and quietly turned the screw in the clamp about half a turn. After five minutes, he came back to Tommy's seat and turned the screw another half turn. After two more turns, Tommy suddenly awoke, gasping for air. He couldn't breathe, and the pain brought tears to his eyes. He fumbled with the clamp, loosening the screw until he could get it off his nose. It was a little sadistic but very funny! I don't know if he ever found out how it happened.

There were some pretty heavy drinkers in Charlie's band. Number one was Charlie Russo. Charlie played lead alto and was the road manager. He was built like a bull but was really a softy. He and I became very close friends. (In fact, he is godfather to my oldest daughter.)

I was drinking quite a bit at that time, but I always felt I had it under control. I drank before, during, and after the job but never let it affect my playing until one day.

We were playing a two-week engagement at the Capitol Theatre in New York, and our first show was at 10:00 a.m. One morning, the ringing of the phone woke me from a booze-induced sleep. It was Russo calling from the theater, telling me the first show was to start in fifteen minutes. I jumped out of bed, threw on my band uniform, ran into the elevator and out of the hotel onto Forty-eighth Street. It was only three blocks to the theater, so I decided to run up Eighth Avenue, the shortest way to the stage door. On the corner of Forty-eighth Street and Eighth Avenue was a chili joint that we frequented. As I rounded the corner, the heavy odor of chili hit me! I lost it and immediately threw up in the gutter.

I made it to the theater just in time to go on stage. After a short version of the theme, we went into a swinging, up-tempo Manny Albam arrangement called "Curtain Time" that ended on a high F for me. So far so good. Next, Charlie introduced Tommy Lynn whose first number was a medium-tempo tune called "I've Got Five Dollars." Still, so far so good. Tommy's next number was a slow ballad, I don't remember the title, but the trumpets didn't come in until the second eight bars of the first chorus, playing whole notes (we called them footballs) in fiberglass derby hats that helped soften the sound.

The sound coming from the bell of my horn began to quiver like Eartha Kitt's vibrato. *Wu wu wu wu.* I couldn't control it, and I began to sweat profusely. This was my first experience with the shakes! (But not my last.)

Ordinarily, if I woke up with a hangover, I would go to the bar and have a cold Ballantine ale or two to settle my stomach before breakfast. I didn't have time to do that this day, but immediately after the first show, I headed across the street to Beefsteak Charles's to quiet my nerves. By the second show, everything was under control again.

We had some real characters in Charlie's band. Bob Carter, the piano player, and Russ Motcalm, the third trumpet player, were roommates. Anytime we had a night off, they would go to their room, take all the water glasses and mirrors, anything made out of glass, and set it out in the hallway. Then they would start drinking, and soon they would begin to fight. We never knew what they fought about, but it happened every time. The next day, they were all buddy-buddy again.

That summer, Charlie bought new uniforms for the band—lightweight single-breasted brown suits with floppy green-and-white bebop ties. We wore them every night for months. The material was very thin and couldn't take much wear. My roommate Buddy Yannon's pants gave way at the knee and exposed the white flesh underneath. Buddy's solution was to take brown shoe polish and smear it all over his knee so you couldn't see his white skin.

About this time, Charlie and Irene decided to get married. Irene wanted to get off the road, having spent several years with Gene Krupa's band before Charlie and settle down.

Irene was not a warm person. Being the bandleader's girlfriend and then wife, she wasn't considered one of the boys. It bothered me when on occasion she would mock Charlie, calling him names like Apple Head, but he loved her.

Charlie had a beautiful home in Hastings-on-Hudson in Westchester County, New York. Quite often, if we had a day off, Charlie would invite the whole band to his home for a party. Irene was a very good cook, especially when she made barbecue ribs, which took some doing to feed sixteen guys.

On one occasion, Charlie invited just Russo and me. Russo rented a car, I didn't even have a driver's license at that time, and we left Manhattan about two in the afternoon. Halfway to Hastings, Russo said, "Let's stop for a drink." We found a nice neighborhood bar that had a shuffleboard table and decided to play a few games. We kept drinking and playing and got involved in a tournament with some of the local patrons. Before we knew it, it was 11:00 p.m. We never got to Charlie's house. Driving back to Manhattan in the condition we were in, I find it amazing that we were neither killed nor arrested! Irene had prepared a large pan of ribs just for the two of us. She never forgave us.

In 1950, very few record companies were interested in recording dance bands, but Charlie signed a contract with London Records. I think it was a British-based company, but you could buy the records in the United States. These were still '78s. (We used to say they weren't released, they escaped!)

At one of the record sessions, we were to record a song called "There's No Tomorrow," actually it was "'O Sole Mio" with English lyrics with a vocal by the Star Dreamers, a vocal group hired just for the recording; they didn't travel with us.

After the intro, Charlie soloed beautifully for sixteen bars. After the vocal, the last chorus started with a rich full ensemble with Charlie playing an obbligato under the melody. My first note started on a high C. I took a deep breath and laid into it. After the first take, the engineer in the control booth said, "Charlie, were getting too much of you, go back and stand beside the trumpet section." We took a second take. "Charlie, still too much, have the trumpets stand." Take three. "Charlie, go stand behind the trumpet section." I was getting frustrated! I was giving as much volume as I could. Take four. "Perfect!" Charlie had this beautiful sound that cut through everything, and the record turned out great.

We recorded about twenty sides for the London label. I still have all but one of those records. Wouldn't you know it? It was the only one on which I had a four-bar solo!

When Bob Carter, our piano player, left to go with Jimmy Dorsey, Charlie hired a young, seventeen-year-old kid from New York. Bob Alberti. He seemed to fit in nicely, playing good solos and accompaniment behind singers. Whenever we played a string of one-nighters in New England, we always seemed to wind up at the Holyoke arena in Holyoke, Massachusetts, after traveling all night to get there. We never checked in a hotel in Holyoke, but always continued on to New York after the job.

During the week, the Holyoke arena provided boxing for the locals. Once in a while, they would bring in a name band and three or four vaudeville acts for a ninety-minute show.

After driving all night, we would have a 10:00 a.m. rehearsal to run over the music for the acts. This day, we were rehearsing the music for a dog act when Charlie noticed that Alberti wasn't playing. He stopped the band and asked, "Bob, don't you have the music?"

"Yes, Charlie, I have it."

Charlie asked, "Why aren't you playing?"

"I can't read music, Charlie." Bob replied

We were stunned! I will complete the Bob Alberti saga later. Sometimes there might be a comedian like Smiley Burnette (Gene Autry's sidekick) or Billy Gilbert, famous for his sneeze, as one of the performers. The shows started about noon and wound up around 11:00 p.m. It was a long day. The balcony ran around the arena in a complete circle, so you had people sitting above and behind you. The show better be good, or you became a target! There were four bars in the arena, which we visited between each show, so by 11:00 p.m., we were feeling pretty good.

It was 150 miles from Holyoke to New York City, and as I said before, there were no interstates or thruways, just two-lane roads. We got the bus packed by eleven thirty and, believe it or not, made it to Charlie's Tavern before closing time!

We had a few days off before we hit the road again and heard that Charlie had hired a new girl singer. Irene had seen her on a local television show and recommended her to Charlie. Her name was Lynn Roberts, and she was fifteen years old. I thought to myself, *How can a fifteen-year-old kid know anything about singing with a big band?*

The following morning, we were to leave on a Southern tour starting in Fayetteville, North Carolina. The bus was parked in front of the President Hotel, waiting for everyone to show up when a car pulled up behind the bus, and this cute blonde with a long ponytail got out of the car, followed by an elderly gentleman, her father. He had a long conversation with Charlie Russo then shook hands, kissed his daughter good-bye, and watched her get on the bus. Russo put her in the front seat then took his seat across the aisle.

From that first night in Fayetteville, I could see Lynn didn't have the maturity or polish of an Irene Daye, but her natural talent and youthful exuberance made up for the lack of experience, which would come. Everyone liked her and soon accepted her as one of the guys, but with respect! She had a young-girl crush on Tommy Lynn, but that eventually turned into a close friendship that lasted for years.

Lynn stayed with the band for close to two years until she was offered a job with the Vincent Lopez Orchestra at the Taft Hotel in New York. Several girl singers came and went. Pat Collins, Peggy King (who later married Andre Previn), and Eileen Rogers, a girl with a very husky voice probably because she smoked cigars.

One day, Charlie told us we were going to record a promotional record for Eveready batteries to a song entitled "Every Cat Has Nine Lives." I guess if you bought a pack of batteries, you got this record free.

We got to the studio, set up, and started to rehearse the arrangement. It was an up-tempo tune, which was not Eileen's forte, plus the fact that she couldn't read music and couldn't seem to learn the melody. After an hour or so, Spivak and Russo decided to call Lynn at home and ask her if she could please come to the studio and help us out.

We stalled until she got there. Russo diplomatically sent Eileen out for lunch. We ran down the arrangement for Lynn just once, and she nailed it perfectly on the first take!

Ironically, a few years later, Eileen made a single record on her own that did rather well. (Go figure!)

In 1950, we did one television show from New York called the *Cavalcade of Bands*. The premise being four different bands seated on this large turntable, which rotated every fifteen minutes to feature the band that would be on camera. I remember we had to wear blue shirts instead of white, and the bell of our instrument was sprayed with a dulling spray to cut down the reflection that could cause a black flare on the TV screen. The show was canceled after thirteen weeks.

The interest in big bands had started to wane after World War II, and by 1951, many ballrooms had closed, and small-town theaters no longer ran stage shows. The booking offices were having a hard time providing steady work for a band on the road. Spivak decided we needed to do more than just play arrangements, so he got this brilliant idea to put on an impromptu show before intermissions. He somehow found out that I knew how to tap dance, so he asked Manny Albam to write an original arrangement for me entitled "In Flew the Flea." My roommate Buddy Yannon would sing the first chorus, and then I would jump down from the trumpet section and go into my dance.

A tap routine usually consisted of eight dance steps that required two choruses (sixty-four bars of music) after which I was to go back to the trumpet section and finish out the arrangement. Now remember, I hadn't danced for twelve years! Charlie called a rehearsal to put together this show he had in mind. We started with "In Flew the Flea." Buddy fumbled through the lyrics on the first chorus, and I jumped down ready to do my Fred Astaire! When I finished my dance, I crawled back up to the trumpet section totally exhausted and out of breath, not being able to pick up my horn and finish the arrangement. Charlie's comment was, "I need a first trumpet player instead of a tap dancer!" Thankfully, that was the end of "In Flew the Flea."

One night at the end of a short tour, Charlie called a meeting to inform us that he could no longer provide enough work to keep the band on salary, and from now on, we would only be working weekends out of New York. At this point, my salary was $150 a week, so Charlie said he would guarantee me three nights at $30 per night. Better than nothing!

I thought this might be a good time to try to get a local 802 union card. To get an 802 card, you had to transfer from your home local, live within the jurisdiction of local 802, not be allowed to work a steady job, only single engagements, and not work outside the jurisdiction of 802. A union representative could show up at your address at any time to confirm that you lived there and were still in town. I found a cheap room over the marquee of a hotel on the corner of Seventy-ninth Street and Columbus Avenue; and for the next six months, I continued to do weekends with Charlie, and fortunately, no one from the union ever checked to make sure I was in town. (I got the card!)

One Monday morning, I received a phone call that was to point my life in another direction!

CHAPTER ELEVEN

"I'm Getting Sentimental over You" (First Chorus)

The Monday-morning phone call was from the Tommy Dorsey office asking if I could be available to go to Mahanoy City, Pennsylvania, that afternoon to substitute for Buddy Childers, Tommy's first trumpet player who had cut his lip in a minor car accident, and how much per night did I want. I said I was available, and I would do it for (I pushed it a little bit) $35 a night. Tommy's manager said okay, but I would have to leave right now, come by the office in the Brill building to pick up the money for the train fare, that the train was leaving at noon from Penn Station, and someone would pick me up when I got there and drive me to the ballroom.

I had a little hangover, but I figured I could tough it out for one day. I picked up the train fare, got to Penn Station, and made the train with twenty minutes to spare.

It was only 145 miles from New York to Mahanoy City, but this was a local that stopped at every railroad crossing along the way. It took seven hours, and by the time I got there, I was pretty frazzled! A nice lady was waiting for me and drove me to the ballroom. It was now seven thirty, and the job started at eight o'clock. I had heard a lot of stories about what an ogre Tommy Dorsey could be, which didn't help my nerves any. Babe Fresk, a tenor saxophone player that I knew only slightly, looked at me and said, "Come with me." He took me behind the bandstand and handed me a pint of Seagram's 7 and a bottle of Coke. "You look like you could use this." I took three deep swallows, chased it with the Coke, and by the time I got on the bandstand, I had no fear. I couldn't believe I was sitting next to Charlie Shavers, a trumpet player that I had admired for years, and in the sax section was Sam Donahue, one of the best jazz saxophone players in the business.

Tommy beat off the first tune, and the sound that came out of that band was wonderful! I could do no wrong. That night was as good as I ever played in my life. At the end of the second set, Nick DiMayo, one of the trombone players, turned around and said to Charlie, smilingly, "How is the kid doing?" Shavers grunted and said, "I wish this motherfucker would make a mistake so I'd know he's human!" What a compliment! Just before intermission, Tommy introduced each guy in the band, and when he got to me, he said to the audience, "This is this young man's first night with the band, but the way he's playing, I feel as though he's been here a long time!"

We played the next night, I don't remember where, then rode the band bus back to New York. The next day, Wednesday, we were featured on the Kate Smith television show. The band had a few days off, and Buddy Childers recovered and came back to the band.

Spivak's band had three jobs that weekend. One at a VFW lodge, one at a tobacco warehouse, and one at an Elks Lodge. (to our departed brothers.) somehow things didn't seem the same. The life had gone out of the band, including Charlie.

When I got back to my hotel on Monday morning, I had a message from Tino Barzie, Dorsey's road manager, asking me to call him. I returned his call, and he told me that Buddy Childers was giving his notice, and would I be available to join the band in California in two weeks at $175 per week. I said I would call him back in two days. I honestly wasn't sure how I felt. I was very comfortable with Spivak, my friends were there, and I was hoping things would get better for the band. I had to talk to Charlie about it. We had a date the next day, so on the way, I asked Charlie if I could sit with him to ask his advice. I told him about the Dorsey offer, but that I didn't know what to do. He didn't hesitate. "There's nothing to think about. That's a great band, and that's where you belong." I have great respect for that man, and we remained good friends for years.

I called Tino and accepted the job. He told me to go by the office and pick up my plane ticket to California and that I would be joining the band for a two-week engagement at the Hollywood Palladium. I went by the Dorsey office and met Vinnie Carbone, who was now Dorsey's personal manager (Another Italian!), and the beginning of another long friendship. I picked up the plane ticket and was told on arrival to check in to the Vine

Lodge Motel in Hollywood. This would be my first trip to the West Coast, and I was pretty excited!

After landing at LAX (Los Angeles International Airport), I hailed a cab and headed for the Vine Lodge Motel. As we pulled up to the motel, I noticed the band bus parked at the curb and several guys milling around on the sidewalk dressed in an assortment of baseball attire—T-shirts, some baseball pants or Levi's, and baseball caps. One guy was waving at me, I recognized Tino Barzie, to come over to the bus. We shook hands, and Tino said, "Can you play softball?" I said, "Sure."

"We have a game with the Harry James band, can you play third base?"

Now, I had played a lot of softball in Pittsburgh when I was with the band at the radio station, and my position was third base. I was what was known as a spray hitter, I didn't hit for power, but I could hit to all fields, and I rarely struck out. Tino said, "Put your stuff in your room and get back here, we leave in fifteen minutes." I certainly wasn't dressed for a ball game. Slacks, a sports shirt, and loafers! We got to the ball field and began some infield practice. I was holding my own at third base, and Sam Hyster, the bass trombone player and team manager, gave me a thumbs-up!

Two station wagons pulled up to the field and out came the Harry James softball team. They all had matching uniforms and shirts with the Harry James Orchestra logo on them. I knew that Harry was an avid baseball fan, he liked the St. Louis Cardinals, and I figured his softball team would wipe us out.

Both Tommy and Harry pitched for a couple of innings and then left. Going into the seventh inning, we were tied 4-4. I got a double; and Tino, the only left-handed batter we had, hit a line drive over the first baseman's head and drove me and from second with the winning run. Harry's band didn't score in the bottom of the seventh, and we won 5-4!

That night, Harry sent a telegram to Tommy at the Palladium, which Tommy read to the audience, quote, "Dear Tom, congratulations on your win today. Would you consider a trade? A new set of mutes and three arrangements for your third baseman!"

That night, Tino told me Tommy wanted me to look over the arrangement of "Well Git It!" and when would I be ready to do it.

I had that record, a great trumpet duet between Ziggy Elman and Ray Wetzel, and that I was sure I could do it the next night. I looked over the first trumpet part and counted the high Fs, twelve of them! Of course I was nervous, but once we started and I realized I was sharing this with Charlie Shavers, I was thrilled! (Dreams do come true.)

One night, Tommy announced that we would be recording the next day. He needed to record four sides to finish out his contract with Decca Records. The four songs we recorded were instrumentals arranged by Bill Finnigan.

Charlie Shavers showed up at the studio wearing white Bermuda shorts, a green silk shirt, white kneesocks, white shoes, and a white cap. (How sharp can you get!)

He brought a friend with him, John Kirby, the leader of the John Kirby quintet that Charlie had played with when he was seventeen years old. Sadly, John Kirby passed away three weeks later.

I also got to meet Conrad Gazzo, the number one trumpet player on the West Coast who had stopped by to say hello to Charlie and some other friends in the band.

One night after work, George Cherb, one of the other trumpet players, and I were walking back to the motel. It was a beautiful, balmy night, and the air smelled sweet.

On the corner of Yucca and Vine, we passed an open-air lunch wagon. The smell of hamburgers and onions was too hard to resist. We sat on a couple of stools and ordered.

Someone sat down on the stool next to me, and I heard a voice that sounded familiar but with a stutter. "Gi-gi-gi-give me a hamburger." I turned to look. It was Fuzzy Knight, a cowboy character actor that I had seen in many Western movies. My thought was, *I guess I'm really in Hollywood!*

We finished the Palladium date and started a string of one-nighters headed back East.

A one-nighter with Tommy was not easy. Every gig was four hours, eight to twelve, or nine to one. We played the first two hours pretty much nonstop then took a half-hour intermission and finished up the last hour and a half except that Tommy always played overtime. (I found out that once in a while Tommy would pop an upper and feel like playing beyond the closing time.) One night, he caught Tak Tavorian looking at his watch. Tommy started hitting Tak's wrist with the end of his trombone slide, trying to break Tak's watch.

"You got no place to go until I tell you!" Tommy growled. I began to see this side of Tommy Dorsey.

As I said before, Tommy used to introduce each member of the band to the audience before an intermission. One night during an engagement at the Edgewater Beach Hotel in Chicago, during the introductions, he got around to Eddie Grady, the drummer. His introduction was, "Folks, I know you've heard of two-beat drummers and four-beat drummers, Eddie is a deadbeat drummer! Take a bow, El Goof-oo!" He could be mean.

I wouldn't say Tommy was a perfectionist, but he certainly knew what he wanted musically. He always gave 100 percent of himself and expected no less from the guys he hired. There was a certain pride being with the Dorsey band because you knew that as long as you stayed there, you were doing your job because if you weren't, you wouldn't be around very long.

If on occasion you went for a high note and missed it, he would never say a word. But if you came in early on a phrase or missed an articulation, you would hear, "Stop goofin'."

Sometimes, after two or three weeks of one-nighters with no night off, things might get a little lax, and guys would lose concentration, and there would be more mistakes than usual. Then came the "Okay, you guys want a goof, I'll show you how to goof! I'm not signing your checks this week! I'm goofin'." Then every night on the bandstand, "See, I'm still goofin'." Tino would wind up bailing everyone out of the hotels until Tommy relented.

Eddie Grady was replaced by Jackie Mills, a fine drummer from California. I had been Eddie's roommate, so Charlie Shavers asked me if I would like to room with him. Charlie and I had become drinking buddies, so I was all for it. Charlie and I always had a bottle between us on the bandstand. Tommy knew it, but as long as we didn't screw up, he didn't say anything.

I knew that in the south, we would experience discrimination, but I was surprised to learn it existed even in the north. When we would check in to a hotel, I would always sign us in at the desk while Charlie, being black, waited by the elevator. We never ate in the hotel dining room but would either go out or order room service. Charlie figured he just didn't want any hassles.

One time however, we were to play at a place called "The Club" outside of Birmingham, Alabama. We got there early, and the band boy, Bibs Mosler, was setting up the bandstand when a heavyset dowager, apparently the head of the committee, said to Tommy, "Mr. Dorsey, is that colored gentleman with y'all?" Tommy answered, "Yes, he's one of my trumpet players." She asked quietly, "Do you think you could give him the night off?" Tommy turned around and hollered to Bibs, "Pack it up, we're leaving!" Apparently flustered, the dowager stuttered, "Mr. Dorsey, Mr. Dorsey, what are you doing?" TD said, "If he doesn't work, we don't work." That ended it, and she backed off. Of course, Charlie was the hit of the evening due to his great playing and entertaining.

My drinking was becoming more prevalent (but also the hangovers!). One night during intermission, I saw Shavers talking to a couple of young girls. When we got back on the bandstand, Charlie said to me, "I got a couple of chicks for us after the gig." I had a really bad hangover that day, and all I wanted to do was go to bed. I said to Charlie, "I have to beg off, man, I just want to go to sleep." I didn't even want a drink, that's how bad I felt. When I got back to the hotel, I went right to bed. I was awakened by the ringing of the telephone. I looked at the bedside clock. It was 3:00 a.m. I fumbled around in the dark until I found the desk lamp then picked up the phone. A woman's voice said, "This is Western Union. I have a very important message for a Mr. Campbell, is he there?" I answered, "This is Mr. Campbell." She went on, "This is a very important message, you better get a pencil and paper and write this down." I searched through the desk drawer until I found a pencil and a sheet of paper. I picked up the phone. "Okay." She said, "Do you have the pencil?" I said, "Yes."

"Do you have the paper?" A little annoyed, I said, "Yes, I have them both." Shaver's voice came up, "Shove 'em up your ass, motherfucker! Ha ha ha!" (It's a lot funnier now than it was then.)

After three or four months of one-nighters, some guys, mostly drinkers, became afflicted with a condition known as telephone-itis, the symptoms usually appearing after work while drinking alone in your hotel room, and this sudden compulsion would arise to call someone you assumed was just waiting to hear from you around 2:00 or 3:00 a.m.

The unfortunate recipient of my affliction was Lynn Roberts, especially when the phone in her house was in her mother's bedroom! This certainly didn't endear me to Lynn's parents after the third or fourth time.

I don't remember why, but Tommy and Charlie Shavers got into an argument one night, and Tommy fired him, which was not unusual; it had happened several times before. The next day, Charlie was gone, and a new trumpet player replaced him that night. His name was Bobby Nichols who I had seen playing with Vaughn Monroe at the Stanley Theater in Pittsburgh when Bobby was sixteen years old.

He was a very good jazz trumpet player, but certainly no Charlie Shavers. I missed my friend and wasn't very happy about him being gone, especially when Nichols would sit down after playing one of Charlie's solos, grab my arm, and ask, "Did you dig the change I played on the fifth bar?" That bugged the hell out of me.

We were working at the Hotel Syracuse in Syracuse, New York, and I was juicing pretty heavily. Up until now, I had never gotten so drunk that I couldn't play, but this night, I crossed the line. I was feeling sorry for myself, and by the last set, I was completely wasted.

After the job, Tino took me aside and asked, "What's the matter, Flea?" In a drunken slur of words, I complained about the trumpet section and brazenly demanded a $100 raise! Tino said he didn't think Tommy would go for that, but he would talk to him; but I didn't wait. That night, I called Charlie Russo and said I wanted to come back to Spivak's band. He said he would talk to Spivak and call me the next day. When he did, he said Charlie said okay but that he couldn't pay me $175 a week. We settled for $163. That night, Tino said Tommy would go for a $25 raise. Being stupid, I said no and gave my notice. The next night, there was a new trumpet player on the bandstand. Billy Marshall from Boston. Tommy told me to let him play the first trumpet book. He did a very good job, so at the end of the night, I asked Tino if Tommy was going to keep him. Tino said, "Yes, he had been hired." I said, "Good, I can go back to New York tomorrow." Tino said, "No, the old man (this is what we called Tommy) wants you on the bandstand every night until you finish out your notice."

After Syracuse, we would be working our way West again, which meant my notice would finish up in Denver, Colorado; and because I quit, I had to pay my own way back to New York. (He taught me a valuable lesson!)

I started working with Spivak again but soon realized I had made a mistake. In the meantime, I called Lynn Roberts, who was working at the Taft Hotel with Vincent Lopez, and asked her out to dinner. She had an afternoon set, so I said I would pick her up about six o'clock. I had a hangover, but I decided not to drink, I didn't want to show up loaded on our first date.

I got to the hotel early (I'm a Virgo), and I was feeling a little nervous. There was a bar in the Taft called the Men's Bar, so I decided to have just one drink to calm me down. I tossed down a whiskey and water and headed for the lobby. I could feel my stomach churning, and I knew I was in trouble. I had spotted a men's room in the lower lobby and made a mad dash for the stairway. I reached the first landing and knew I wouldn't make it. The first thing I saw was a large potted plant, which received the contents of my stomach. Fortunately, there was no one around to witness it. When I met Lynn, she asked why I was sweating!

We went out together a few more times, and I mistakenly began to believe that she was my girlfriend, although our relationship never progressed beyond a friendly good night kiss. Actually, my drinking made her very uncomfortable, but she was too young and too nice to tell me to get lost! In the fifties, things with the Spivak band were just not going well, so when I got a call from Ray Anthony to join his band at the Capitol Theatre on Christmas Eve, I accepted.

CHAPTER TWELVE

"Getting Sentimental over You" (Second Chorus)

I had about three weeks before I joined the Ray Anthony band, so they sent me to a tailor to be measured for a new uniform. Spivak had a few more dates, and I was prepared to work those out. Then Lynn Roberts told me that Tino Barzie had seen her at the Taft and recommended her to Tommy as his new girl singer and that she was joining the band on the road the next day. Now I really knew what a mistake I had made!

Suddenly, out of the blue, I got a phone call from Tino. He said Tommy had heard that I was leaving Spivak to join Ray Anthony, and would I be interested in coming back to the Dorsey band with the $25 raise. I couldn't believe my good fortune. What I didn't know was that when they told Lynn I was coming back, she was worried that I could create a problem because of my drinking and that she might have to quit. Tino assured her they wouldn't let that happen.

I called Ray Anthony exactly two weeks before I was to start, and quit! Understandably, he was furious.

Vinnie Carbone took me to the airport, and I rejoined the band on December 18 in New Orleans at the Roosevelt Hotel.

When I got there, I discovered that Lynn had found a new friend, Gordon Polk, Tommy's other singer, and that they were hanging out together.

Gordon was an affable and good entertainer. He did upbeat tunes sprinkled with comedy, songs such as "Ain't She Sweet" and "Mississippi Mud." I could see why Lynn liked him; I liked him too. I also found out that he was an alcoholic and was a member of Alcoholics Anonymous.

I had become more than fond of Lynn, so I didn't know how to take this situation. By the third night, I was feeling rejected and sorry for myself. That night, after work, I decided to see just how drunk I could get by hitting every bar on Bourbon Street. I wound up in the sixth joint, sitting at the bar and looking at my reflection in a dirty cracked mirror behind the bottles with two mangy drunks, one on either side of me. (It looked like a scene that I had seen many times from the movie *Lost Weekend*.)

I knew I had to get out of there and headed back to my hotel. I picked up the phone in the lobby and called Gordon's room. It was 3:00 a.m. I know I woke him up, but I was desperate. I pleaded, "Please, Gordon, let me come up, I need help!"

He opened the door, wearing only a pair of shorts, and invited me in. I plopped down in an easy chair and looked around the room. The only light was from a small lamp on the bedside table. I noticed some kind of garment on the back of the desk chair. "I guess Lynn left just before I came up," I insinuated. "Lynn wasn't here," he answered. "Oh really," I smirked. Indicating the desk chair, I said, "Then how come she left her panties here?" Gordon picked up the garment, showed it to me, and said, "You mean this?" It was his undershirt! I broke down sobbing. What was happening to me? That goddamn booze was making me see things that weren't there.

Gordon put his arm around me and said, "Come, let's get you to bed, call me when you wake up, and we'll talk about it."

I woke about noon and called him immediately. He asked me to meet him in the lobby. "I want you to come with me," he said.

We hailed a cab and, after a short ride, stopped at a plain-looking building and went inside. I asked Gordon, "Where are we?" "We're at one of the New Orleans chapters of AA," he answered. I certainly had heard about AA but didn't really know much about it. There were quite a few people there, and soon the meeting started.

As I listened to the stories being told, I realized I was not alone with my problem and that there was help available if I was willing to accept it.

When the meeting was over, I gathered up all the pamphlets and literature provided and was eager to learn more. Back at the hotel, I spent the rest of the afternoon learning about AA and admitting to myself that I was (am) an alcoholic.

Being that this was our night off, I called Lynn and asked her if she would like to go to the movies with me. She said she had already promised to go with Gordon. I was disappointed, and later as I was standing on the sidewalk in front of the hotel, I watched them leave together. I figured, "Fuck it." And my first impulse was to head for the nearest bar, but something happened! There was a taxi in front of the hotel; I climbed in and asked the driver if he knew where the AA building was. He did, and I got there in time for the eight o'clock meeting. It was December 21, 1952, and that decision that night saved my life. (As I write this, it has been fifty-four years and ten months without a drink since that night.)

The next week was a nightmare. I was going through withdrawal, and each night on the bandstand was torture. After the third day of not drinking, I awoke about 4:00 a.m. in a panic. I heard this chirping and saw a little bluebird flying around the room. I knew in my conscious mind that they weren't real and that this was the price I had to pay. Trying to play the horn while shaking and sweating was nearly impossible. I knew I wasn't making it, and after a couple of days, I went to Tommy and said I understood if he wanted to let me go. His answer was, "I know what you're going through. It'll pass." I will always be grateful to him for that.

He was right. Little by little, it did pass, and I began to return to normal. We finished the engagement at the Roosevelt Hotel on New Year's Eve and hit the road the next day.

As it turned out, 1953 was to become a very eventful year. After about ten one-nighters, we wound up in Las Vegas, Nevada, for a two-week engagement at the New Frontier Hotel and Casino.

Apparently, Gordon wasn't interested in anything more than a platonic friendship with Lynn, so she and I wound up spending a lot of time together (off the bandstand). I tried not to make it obvious, believing that we shouldn't mix our personal time with business. (The old saying, "You shouldn't shit where you eat!")

The only time I ever came close to slipping back to drinking happened in Las Vegas. One night after work, I assumed Lynn and I would get a bite to eat and maybe take in a lounge show when she told me that Tommy's son Chipper was in town and that she had agreed to meet him after work. I was very upset (Jealousy is not an admirable trait!) I said something stupid and marched off. Once again, I felt hurt and rejected. "I'll show her!" And I headed for the casino bar. I ordered a double Seagram's 7 and water. The bartender sat it in front of me. I just stared at it and could not bring myself to pick it up. *She's not worth it, nothing's worth it!* I turned around and walked out of the bar.

I had just gotten back to the room at our motel when the phone rang. It was Lynn. "Are you all right?" "I'm fine," I answered. "How was your date?" "I told Chipper I had to get back to the motel, I was worried about you." Good things were beginning to happen.

This was my first time in Las Vegas. Vegas was a lot of fun in the early 1950s (not like now). All the casinos were run by the Syndicate. Rooms and food were inexpensive. One casino featured a restaurant in the lobby called the Chinese chuck wagon where you could eat all you wanted for $1.50. You could go into any main showroom and watch the show for free because they knew that eventually you had to pass through the casino. Today, each venue in the casino—the coffee shop, the men's room, the shops—have to pay for themselves.

One night I was standing by one of the craps tables, watching people roll the dice. I knew very little about the odds and what it took to win. We had just gotten our paycheck for the week when one of the trombone players in the band joined the people at the table. Within ten minutes, he lost his whole week's salary! I thought, *How stupid.* Ironically, the next afternoon, Lynn and I happened to be walking through the casino when we saw Tommy Dorsey sitting at the roulette table. I didn't think Tommy was that much of a gambler, so I was curious to see why he was there. He told us that being the headliner at the casino, he was expected to be seen there once in a while. He was playing O and double O, the highest odds on the wheel. We watched for quite a while; all the time, he was losing then suddenly he began to win. He wound up winning $7,000. The next day, he went out and bought a piece of property. Moral—if you want to win, you need to be able to afford to lose until your luck changes.

After Las Vegas, we hit the road again, back and forth across the country. The Dorsey band worked very hard, rarely a night off, always a four-hour gig; and as I said before, Tommy always played overtime.

I must tell you this story.

Tommy's sexual preference was to be the recipient of oral sex. I asked him once if he ever reciprocated. He grunted, "Are you kidding? You'll never catch me cleaning out the pantry!"

We went to Canada for a week of one-nighters, and while there, Tommy met this beautiful Norwegian blonde; let's call her Elsa. He became enamored with her and decided to take her on the road with us. Problem was, she had no passport, so he stashed her in the back of the instrument truck and brought her across the border.

After a couple of weeks, he began to get bored and looked for a way to get rid of her. He instructed Lee Castle to take care of it.

fucked it up! Tommy looked at me and said, "He doesn't play the rest of the night." Anytime Charlie tried to pick up his horn, Tommy would push his arms down with the slide of his trombone. As the night went on, Charlie started to sober up, but Tommy still wouldn't let him play.

The next morning, we were all on the bus getting ready to leave. Tommy decided he would drive the bus, which he did quite often. Shavers came out of the lodge, across the lawn, carrying his suitcase and horn. When he got to the door of the bus, Tommy leaned out and said, "You don't work here anymore," shut the door, and took off. That might seem kind of harsh, but I understood why he did it. As much as I loved Charlie and knew we would miss him, I knew Tommy was right. (Shavers was back a couple of months later.)

The next week once again found us in Hollywood. While there, we made a twenty-minute movie short for Universal called *Dorsey Brothers Encore*. It featured Lynn and Gordon Polk on a couple of numbers and a dancer whose name escapes me. The closing number featured Paul and I dueling on "Well Git It" (although Mickey Mangano and I recorded the soundtrack). In typical Hollywood fashion, instead of being able to just listen and watch the band, they had to have the dancer jumping and twirling in front of the band. (Visual, visual!)

I am reminded of a story I heard about Tommy when they were making a movie in the forties called *DuBarry Was a Lady*. Tommy had some heavy drinkers in the band, and one day when they finished shooting the scenes for that day, the director said, "Okay, Tommy, have the boys back on the set tomorrow morning at 9:00 a.m. Tommy said, "Are you serious? My trumpet section doesn't start to puke until noon!"

The chronological order of events for the next year or so may not be totally accurate, but you must remember that all this happened over fifty years ago!

We began working our way back East to another three-week engagement at the Statler Hotel. One night in Philadelphia, Tommy said to me, "I got this kid I want to hear. Put him between you and Callahan (his Irish name for Cohen) and let him play a couple of tunes." That kid was John Frosk, a trumpet player from Canada who had been working with Al Martino. He was short and stocky and had the thickest glasses I had ever seen. They looked like Coke bottle bottoms.

He had a good sound, great range, but his conception of the Dorsey style was rather corny; apparently, Tommy saw something in him that escaped me at that time. Tommy hired him, and for the next couple of weeks, he sat between Paul Cohen and me in the trumpet section. I must say he was a quick learner, so when Paulie left at the end of the Statler engagement, John took over his chair. Eventually, John settled in New York and is currently playing first trumpet in the long-running Broadway hit *Chicago*.

While at the Statler, we did a segment on Jackie Gleason's *The Honeymooners* show, which led to our becoming the summer replacement for the Gleason show. Tommy also signed a contract with Bell Records, a subsidiary of Pocket Books Inc. These were six-inch, forty-five rpm (revolutions per minute) vinyl records that were sold in supermarkets for $0.39. (You might possibly find one at a flea market today!)

Because of the exposure on the TV show, Tommy negotiated a contract with the Statler Hotel whereby the band would play there six months out of the year, which was unheard-of for a big band at that time.

While at the Statler, Lynn was provided with a room so that she could change into her gown before the job each night, although she stayed at her home in Rego Park. She didn't drive, so her father would pick her up after work.

By now, we were very close, and so near the end of that year, I got up enough courage to propose, and she accepted. (Her father was okay with it, but her mother wasn't too thrilled!) When Lynn told Tommy we were planning to be married, he tried to talk her out of it, telling her that if the girl singer married a musician, it never lasted. (We lasted seventeen years.) We knew we were to have three weeks off in March, so we set our wedding date for March 2, 1954. We invited Tommy, but at that time, he was in Florida attending the New York Yankees spring training.

We both wanted to go some place warm for our honeymoon, so after the reception, we packed the car and headed for St. Petersburg, Florida. For the next ten days, the temperature never rose above the low fifties; and in Florida, that's cold!

Year 1954 was a very busy year for the band. The TV show was now called *Stage Show*, which preceded the Gleason show by half an hour; and after the show, we would pack everything up, get on the bus, and head for Frank Daly's Meadowbrook in New Jersey where we worked from 10:00 till 2:00 a.m. then Monday morning back on the bus for one-nighters until the weekend.

Lynn and I decided that we didn't want to ride the bus anymore, so we bought a nice 1954 Oldsmobile so that we could go on our own.

While at the Statler, we finished up the final thirteen-week segment of the TV show and was scheduled for a bunch of one-nighters from New York to California, the first one being the senior ball at the University of Virginia in Charlottesville. It was over four hundred miles from New York, which meant an all-night drive. Lynn had not gotten her driver's license, so it was up to me to get us there. We finished the Statler engagement on a Saturday night, and after the job, Tommy told me to come to his room before we left. He opened a leather case that was filled with a lot of multicolored pills. He handed me two heart-shaped orange pills and a glass of water. "Here," he said, "take one of these now and keep the other one for later. I want to make sure you get to the job."

We took off about 1:30 a.m. and headed south. That pill sure worked but by 8:00 a.m., it had started to wear off. I thought it would be a good idea to find a motel near the college instead of staying at the hotel in town. Motels at that time were not what they are now, and the one we found was pretty shabby, but we were dog-tired.

We checked in about 9:00 a.m., and since there was no phone in the room, we asked the desk clerk to please have someone knock on our door and wake us at six o'clock.

When I woke up, I couldn't figure out why it was so dark and quiet. I looked at my watch, it said twelve o'clock. There was no daylight coming through the window so twelve o'clock when? It couldn't be noon; then it hit me! We must have slept through the whole job!

Lynn was sitting up in bed, and I hollered, "Get up, get up! We gotta go." She looked at me kind of funny. "Where do you think you're going?" I realized she was right. We couldn't go to the college, the job was over. I remembered seeing a telephone booth next to the motel office, so if I could call the college and get a hold of Tino; I could let him know what happened. Fortunately, they were still packing up after the job, so someone from the college found Tino, and he answered the phone. "Jesus Christ, what happened to you two? We were all worried, not knowing if you had an accident or something!" I assured him we were all right and explained what had happened with the motel.

"Okay, meet us at the next town tomorrow morning. You'll have to talk to the Ol' Man about it."

Needless to say, there was no more sleeping that night! All I could think about was how it must have been with no first trumpet and no girl singer, and how I was going to face Tommy!

We got to the next town and pulled up to the hotel where the band was staying. Someone told me Tommy was in the coffee shop, so in I went. He was sitting in a booth with Tino having breakfast. I went over to the booth and stood there waiting for the tirade I knew was coming. He didn't even look up, but kept on eating. He let me stand there for three or four minutes then without even looking at me, said "Get rid of the fuckin' car!" "Okay, Tom," was all I could say just then.

The next day, I cornered Tino and tried to explain how difficult it would be to get rid of our car, being that we were on our way to California. He said, "Just let it lay low for a couple of days, but be sure you don't fuck up again."

The rest of the tour was uneventful until on the way back from the West Coast during a swing through the southern states. Tommy announced one night that Buddy Rich would be joining the band the following week. We all knew about Buddy's reputation, but I was more excited about hearing him play than his attitude. I must say that the six months or so that he was with the band was one of the musical highlights of my so-called career. I couldn't wait to go to work each night. He inspired me to play over my head.

Lynn and I both got along with Buddy very well. He was very friendly and treated us both with respect.

Along about February of that year, we were to open the new Saxony Hotel in Miami Beach. Most of the band stayed at the Wofford Beach Hotel, but Buddy brought his whole family down—his wife, little girl, his mother and father—and put them up at a very expensive motel. (We found out later that he had the bill sent to Tommy.)

On opening night, Buddy reserved a table for his family right in front of the bandstand. His wife draped her mink coat over the back of her chair.

When Buddy joined the band, Tommy had given him an advance that he was supposed to pay back out of his salary each week but up to now hadn't done so. Tommy had a U.S. Marshal all set to repossess the mink coat in the middle of Buddy's drum solo. Somehow, Buddy got wind of it, and I saw him and Tommy arguing in a corner of the lobby. I guess they settled it, but it would really have been hilarious if it had happened.

It started in Las Vegas. Tommy started bugging Lynn about her ponytail, jokingly at first, but as time went on, he made it obvious that he wanted her to change her hairstyle.

She decided, just to keep the peace, that she would wear her hair up.

While at the Saxony, we were to spend our first wedding anniversary, so that night, Lynn decided to wear her hair down in her ponytail. Tommy got on the bandstand, came back to the trumpet section, and said to me, "I guess she doesn't care what I said about the hair." I tried to explain, "Tonight's our first anniversary, Tom, and she just wanted to wear it down for tonight." "Well, after tonight, she can wear it anyway she wants, she's through!" Once again, I gave Tino my two weeks' notice.

CHAPTER THIRTEEN

Cuba/Copa

The band left Miami, but we decided to stay a little while longer. A friend of ours, Dr. Joe Groom, invited us to stay at his house in the Florida Keys. Plus we needed some time to figure out what we were going to do once we got back to New York.

We decided that Lynn would try to make it as a single and that I would be her conductor. We asked Manny Albam, who happened to be my best man at our wedding, to write the arrangements for Lynn's act.

We contacted some booking agents to get us some work. We started off doing the borscht circuit (hotels in the Catskills) and some other obscure engagements. After being with the wonderful Dorsey band, it was a stretch to work with some of the mediocre musicians, but I learned early on to make the best of it. To criticize guys who were really trying didn't do any good. You could get much more out of them if they were treated with respect.

Then one day, we got a call for a gig in Cuba (before Castro!). We flew to Havana and was told that Lynn would be doing a television show (Cuba's answer to our hit parade) and a stage show at a beautiful Havana theater.

At the first rehearsal, we discovered that no one in the band spoke English, but it wasn't necessary. The music spoke for itself. It was a very good orchestra with a girl drummer, Anna, and they loved playing Manny Albam's arrangements. We all got along just fine except for the piano-playing leader! I was conducting for Lynn, and apparently this bothered the leader who complained to the Cuban musicians' union that it made him lose face in front of his musicians. They called me down to the union office, and since I actually wasn't getting paid to work with Lynn, they said I could no longer conduct, which was okay because the band knew the arrangements by now. (Later, the band confided in me that their leader was a *gigipollas* [asshole]!)

We enjoyed being in Cuba. The people were warm and friendly, and it seemed like a happy country. We had the pleasure of playing there again later that year.

After an engagement at some broken-down club in Illinois and a few single dates around Miami, we returned to New York.

Lynn's parents suggested that we move in with them until we got settled. The kind of money Lynn was getting for her act didn't allow for the extra expense of a conductor, so I felt I needed to work to help take up the slack. It was not easy being a musician in New York. Local 802 had thirty thousand musicians of which three thousand, roughly 10 percent, were gainfully employed.

One afternoon, while hanging around the 802 musicians' union floor, I ran into a trumpet player, Frank Lo Pinto, who had been on the Bob Astor band with me. He was working at the Copacabana and said they were looking for a trumpet player, and would I be interested. The lead alto player, who was acting as the band contractor, called and hired me the next day. Little did I know that this would be the worst job I would ever have in the music business.

The Copacabana was located on East Sixtieth Street and was probably one of the most famous nightclubs in the world. Every big act in show business played there. Great singers like Tony Bennett, Vic Damone, and Sammy Davis Jr. Wonderful comedians such as Joe E. Lewis and Jimmy Durante. Dean Martin and Jerry Lewis played their last engagement as a team at the Copa.

Actually, the Copacabana was the basement of the Hotel Fourteen. (Jimmy Durante used to liken it to a coal mine, remarking, "If John L. Lewis, the president of the coal miners union, knew we was workin' here, he'd t'row us all out!")

It was common knowledge that the Copa was owned by the Syndicate. Once in a while, I would notice one or two of the more well-known underworld figures sitting at their private table to the right of the bandstand.

The Copa was managed by a pig of a man named Jules Podell, and he ran it with an iron fist. It was not uncommon to see him punch a waiter for some imagined infraction. One night, on the way to the band room from the bandstand, I saw him shove a plate of Chinese food in his wife's face.

Musicians were not allowed to be in the club except to go to and from the bandstand. We were not allowed to use the men's room. If you needed to piss, you had to use the men's room in the lobby of the Hotel Fourteen. Once in a while, the management of the hotel and the Copa would have a falling-out, and we would be barred from using the hotel facilities. (I tried pissing on the sidewalk, hoping to be arrested to draw attention to our working conditions.) The doorman at the Copa had a working arrangement with the local police. There was no parking on Sixtieth Street or surrounding streets, so when the doorman parked a customer's car, he would put a book of Copa matches on the dashboard so the police wouldn't ticket it. I used to watch the patrol cars pull up to the entrance of the Copa to be paid off by the doorman.

The only union help at the Copa were the musicians and entertainers. No union rep ever dared to set foot in the club. The bandleader was a half-assed trombone player by the name of Mike Durso, a coward who was scared to death of Jules Podell. We literally had no one on our side. From Monday to Thursday, we worked from 7:30 to 3:00 a.m., playing dance sets and two shows. On Friday and Saturday, the hours were 8:00 until 4:00 a.m. with dance sets and three shows, all this for $153 bucks a week. Usually after the last show, everyone would have left the club, but we would have to sit on the bandstand and play until the last minute while the janitor cleaned the dance floor.

I detested that job and began to wonder if this was all the music business had in store for me. I thought about doing something else, but what? I had always liked photography, but I knew to be good at it, I had to learn it the right way. I enrolled at the New York Institute of Photography and signed up for a commercial course. Classes started at 9:00 a.m. and ended at four in the afternoon. The school was on East Thirty-third Street, so I had to take the subway to Manhattan early in the morning and back to Queens in the afternoon, a quick dinner then drive back to Manhattan to be at the Copa by seven o'clock. (It was still possible to find a parking space on the street at night in those days.)

Soon this routine started to take its toll. I found myself catnapping between the shows and dance sets. Then one night when I was really beat, one of the guys gave me a Dexamyl, a mild upper that helped get rid of the fatigue. He introduced me to his friend, a trombone player, whose brother worked at a pharmaceutical house and could get these pills for five cents apiece. It wasn't long before I was hooked. I would get a box of a hundred on Monday, and by Thursday, I would be calling for another hundred. It was a terrible addiction, and it took many months for me to kick the pill habit after I left the Copa.

I did finish the course at the photography school and some time later took another one in portraiture. For a short time, while playing in Broadway shows, I actually made a few bucks doing professional photos for some of the actors. (Actors aren't too swift about paying though!)

Lynn was still doing an occasional engagement out of town. One night while working at the Chez Paree nightclub in Montréal, Canada, who should walk in but Mr. Dorsey. He told her the band was set to do a show at the Paramount Theatre in New York with Frank Sinatra and would she like to come back with the band; not that he'd like to have Lynn back with the band, but would she want to come back. She said okay and joined the band a month later. Tommy was all set with the trumpet section, so there wasn't any place for me then. Jack Laubach, a very good lead player, was heading the section. When Tommy got back to New York, I met with him in the barbershop at the Piccadilly Hotel where he told me Laubach would be leaving after the Paramount gig and that I could come back with the band if I wanted to. And so I did.

CHAPTER FOURTEEN

"Getting Sentimental over You" (Out Chorus)

After the Paramount engagement, the band commuted in and out of New York until the TV show finished in late September then back to the Statler until the end of the year. Early in November, Tommy threw a party at his home in Greenwich, Connecticut. It was a beautiful fall day, so everything was set up outdoors. He invited the whole band, plus some other guests, including Bert Parks (of the Miss America pageant fame) who was also his next-door neighbor. The only person he didn't invite was his soon-to-be-divorced-wife, Janie. We could see her watching from an upstairs window.

By now, Lynn and I had moved into our own apartment in Astoria, Queens, overlooking LaGuardia Airport. It was there that we got the shocking phone call that Tommy had died the morning of November 26, 1956. As I remember, the strongest feeling I had was one of disbelief. Every night, through the remainder of the Statler engagement, with Jimmy leading the band, I found myself constantly glancing toward the entrance of the Café Rouge, fully expecting Tommy to walk in.

I have been asked if I thought that there was a possibility that Tommy might have committed suicide. *No way!* I remember a recent conversation with him whereby he told me he was looking ahead about doing another TV show. But this time, he stated, "The band would not be just the backup for the acts!"

Before we finished the Statler gig, Jimmy asked Lynn and I if we would please stay with the band when it left town. Actually, we had just found out that Lynn was pregnant and had decided that it was time to get off the road.

Also, I felt, without Tommy, it just wouldn't be the same. He was the leader, the boss, and the driving force that made the band what it was. I have worked with many bandleaders since, but none have had the lasting effect on me as did Tommy Dorsey.

2nd row left, my mother with flute
3rd. row left, my father with cornet

me age three, 1927

Fishing camp—our summer mansion

"The Dancing Campbells'"
Lt. to rt. Jack, Ronnie, Me, Mother

"A Hot Duo", 1940

"Peabody High School" band, 1941

Bob Astor band, 1943

Corporal Campbell

"B" band brass section

"B" band radio show

"A" band New Years Eve, 1945

Tony Pastor Orch. Pnnsylvania Hotel, 1946

The Clooney Sisters, Rosemary and Betty

Charlie Spivak

Charlie Spivak Orch. Capitol Theatre, 1950

"Happy days at the Croydon bar"
Lt. to rt. Me, Charlie Russo, Buddy Yannon, Rusty Nichols

Tommy Dorsey. "Flea", Jimmy Dorsey

Tommy Dorsey Orch. Hollywood Palladium, 1951

T.D. Orch., Statler Hotel, NYC 1952

Intermission, lt. to rt. P. Cohen, Unknown, C. Shavers, Flea, J. Mills,
L. Shineman, T. Dorsey

Dorsey trpt. Section, "Bitsy" Mullins, John Frosk, "Flea", Lee Castle

"Flea" Solos!

Non pressure! J. Amoroso, J.McCormick, Flea, L. Castle, D. Mettome

Impromtu jam session at Utah State Prison Jimmy Henderson, Tak Tkvorian, Teddy Lee, Flea

On the set of "Dorsey Bros. Encore" 1953
Jimmy Dorsey, Julie Dorsey, Tommy Dorsey

"Happy Birthday", Tommy, 'Mom' Dorsey, Jimmy

(Last known photo of Dorsey band-three weeks
Before Tommy's death) Photo by, Flea 1956

"One Lucky Guy", March 2, 1954

****   THE "FABULOUS DORSEYS"   ****

****   TOMMY   DORSEY   ORCHESTRA - featuring - JIMMY DORSEY   ****

DAY	DATE	CITY	LOCATION	HOTEL	TIME
AUGUST:					
	17 - 30	Las Vegas, Nev.	Last Frontier Hotel	Desert Spa	House policy
Mon	31	Stockton, Cal.	Katten-Marengo Store	Stockton	6 - 9
SEPTEMBER					
Tue	1	Winnemucca, Nev.	Sonona Inn	enroute	9 - 1
Wed	2	Boise, Ida.	Miramar Ballroom	Boise	9 - 1
Thur	3	Burley, Ida.	Y-Del Ballroom	enroute	9 - 1
Fri	4	Salt Lake City, U.	Lagoon Amuse. Park	Newhouse	9 - 1
Sat	5	Salt Lake City, U.	Lagoon Amuse. Park	Newhouse	9 - 1
Sun	6	Salt Lake City, U.	Hill US AF - Ogden,U.	Newhouse	9 - 1
Mon	7	Salt Lake City, U.	Lagoon Amuse. Park	enroute	9 - 1
Tue	8				
Wed	9			enroute Denver	
Thur	10	Colorado Sprgs.Col.	Hiawatha Gardens	Albany Hotel	9 - 1
Fri	11-13	Denver, Col.	Lakeside Park	Albany (enroute Sun. eve.)	
Sat.& Sun.		Fri 8:30-12:30***Sat. 8:30-1:00***Sun. Mat.2:30-5:30 & 8:30-12:30***			
Mon	14	Rapid City, S.D.	Ellsworth USAF	Alex Johnson	8 - 12
Tue	15	Scottsbluff, Neb.	Terrytown Arena	enroute	9 - 1
Wed	16	Hays, Kan.	Ft.Hays State College	Lamer Hotel	7-8:15 & 8:45 - 12:30
Thur	17			enroute Fargo,N.D.	
Fri	18	Halstad, Minn.	Legion Rec. Center	Gardner Hotel in Fargo,N.D. enroute	9 - 1
Sat	19	Winnipeg,Manitoba	Rancho Don Carlos	Ft. Garry	House policy
thru	25	(Canada)	1 week-enroute nite of 25th		
Sat	26	Duluth,Minn.	Armory	Duluth Hotel	9 - 1
Sun	27	Breckenridge,Minn.	Legion Pavilion		9 - 1
Mon	28				
Tue	29	New Ulm,Minn.	Georges' Ballroom		9 - 1
Wed	30	Austin, Minn.	Terp Ballroom		8:30 - 12:30

****

No night off!

CHAPTER FIFTEEN

Jingles/Jungle

One night while at the Statler, Lynn received a note from a man by the name of Chuck Goldstein, inviting her to join him and his wife at their table.

Chuck Goldstein was one of the original Modernaires, the wonderful vocal group made famous with the Glenn Miller Orchestra. He told Lynn that he and his partner, Bob Swanson, had started a company called GoldSwan Productions producing radio and TV commercials known as jingles. He liked Lynn's voice and thought she would do well as a lead singer with his vocal group. At the time, she had no idea what a jingle singer was but said she would give it a try.

Good jingle singers were rare. They had to come into the studio and read the music at sight even the harmony parts. Lynn did not read music, but she had this uncanny ability to hear a melody line just once and then sing it. For the next twenty years, she became one of the top jingle singers in New York!

In the meantime, it was back into the New York jungle for me. My friend Dick Perry, a trumpet player that had been on the Dorsey band, recommended me to replace Paul Cohen in the pit at the Roxy Theatre. (The enlisted man's version of Radio City Music Hall.)

The Roxy Orchestra was very good, and I enjoyed playing the shows. It was a full-time job—four shows a day, six days a week—but once again after a year, we got the notice that it was closing and that the theatre would be torn down.

During my stay at the Roxy, a wonderful thing happened. On August 13, 1957, Lynn and I were blessed with our first child, a beautiful daughter, Darla Juda Campbell.

Soon after, I received a phone call from my friend Johnny Perilli, a drummer, who had replaced Bobby Ricky on the Spivak band.

Johnny was out of town with a show called *Music with Mary Martin,* and the first trumpeter had quit in the middle of the tour, and could I join them in Milwaukee?

It was a very pleasant experience. The very talented Ms. Martin did excerpts from the Broadway shows in which she had starred, including flying as Peter Pan. She carried two male dancers and a brilliant Brazilian guitar player by the name of Luis Bonfa who has since become a star in his own right. The music was very good under the direction of Mary's conductor, Johnny Lesko, and we became friends. John told me that Mary was scheduled to star in a new Broadway show sometime in the future and that he was hoping to be the conductor, and if so, I was sure to have a job. (More about this later.)

Back in the jungle again. A short stint at the Latin Quarter, another sewer, even though it was on the second floor, a brief time with the show band at the Plaza Hotel until Jerry Kail and I got fired for laughing at the conductor, some dates with a Latin band Vincentico Valdez up in the Bronx from 11:00 to 3:00 a.m., and then a call from ex-Copa bandleader Mike Durso who had a small show band at a real sewer called Jack Silverman's Café on Broadway, right next to Birdland.

It wasn't as bad as the Copa, just depressing! (At least we could use the men's room!)

One night, after we finished, Mike Durso called a meeting of the band in the back room, and true to his colors began whining about how business was declining at the club and that we should be grateful to the management for keeping us employed, and wouldn't it be a nice gesture if we would forgo the money for the previous week's rehearsal and overtime. He took a vote, and after the rest of the band grudgingly accepted, I said, "No!"

After the rest of the band had gone, he informed me of my two weeks' notice. As I came out of the club, I saw Hy Small, the other trumpet player, talking to a guy who looked kind of familiar to me. Hy asked me what Mike had said to me after the meeting, so I told him I had received my notice. The gentleman talking to Hy asked me if I knew the reason. I said I assumed it was because I wouldn't kick back the rehearsal and overtime money. It seems this gentleman was a member of the board of local 802 and said Mike Durso couldn't do that and that I could bring him up on charges. Which I did!

We all received a letter from the union requesting our presence at a meeting of the board two weeks later. All the guys in the band confirmed what I had said about Mike's meeting and about giving back the rehearsal and overtime money. When I went before the board and stated my case, I asked the board to please not punish the rest of the band for agreeing to Mike's coercive suggestion!

Durso and I both received letters from the board, stating that Durso must rescind my notice and could not fire me for any reason without approval of the board!

Ironically, two days later, I got a call from the contractor of a new Broadway show called *Fiorello!* and that I had been recommended by Johnny Lesko and that rehearsal started in a week. Now I had to go to Durso and ask to be let out of the job in less than a week. (He was relieved to get rid of me!)

When I arrived at the first rehearsal of *Fiorello!*, I found my friend Paulie Cohen in the first trumpet chair. This was my first Broadway show, and luckily, I picked a winner.

Fiorello! won the Pulitzer Prize and a Tony Award that year and was a huge hit. We ran for almost three years.

Tom Bosley starred as the legendary Mayor LaGuardia supported by a great character actor Howard Da Silva. I was still very much into photography and got permission to attend the photo shoot a few days after the show opened as long as I stayed out of the way. I used high-speed film, available light, and no flash. When I showed Mr. Da Silva a shot of him I had taken, he was very complimentary and autographed it for me. I took a chance and asked him if after the Wednesday matinee, he would give me five minutes on stage to do a portrait of him. He was very gracious and even invited me to have a steak dinner with him when we finished.

When I approached Tom Bosley with the same request, he farted me off; he didn't want to be bothered!

Now with residuals coming in because of Lynn's commercials and my steady job at the theater, Lynn's father set up a savings plan whereby we soon had enough money for the down payment on a house of our own. For $23,000, we bought a two-story solid brick end unit in Middle Village, Queens. (With a garage in the rear you couldn't get to!) Although a successful Broadway show means steady work, the job itself can be very boring, especially if you are playing an underpart such as second or third trumpet. Six nights a week plus matinees on Wednesday and

Saturday. Physical working conditions left a lot to be desired also. Some of the orchestra pits were very small and crowded. The musicians' area was usually under the stage adjacent to the pit, sparsely furnished, with not much attention given to comfort. On matinee days, with three hours between shows, you could either hike up to Joe Harbor's bar; hang out at Jim & Andy's; or go down to Fort-second Street, have a hot dog (with sauerkraut), and take in a cheap double feature.

During the show, you could catch up on your reading between music cues. On one occasion, I happened to be reading *The Rise and Fall of the Third Reich*, a thick book that had a large picture of a swastika on the cover. One night during intermission, the stage manager came down to the band area, demanding to know who in the pit was reading *Mein Kampf,* Hitler's diary. It seemed someone in the balcony with binoculars had seen the swastika and was very upset.

While doing *Fiorello!*, another blessed event happened. Our second child was born on June 22, 1961, a son, Daryl Jude Campbell.

After a show closed, it didn't necessarily mean you could get another one, especially if you weren't in the stable of two powerful contractors that controlled most of the hiring of theater musicians. The contractors were both mediocre string players that, as rumor had it, both invested in shows years before and had been given jobs as house contractors in some of the major theaters. They were not nice men! Especially Morris Stonzek.

If you were fortunate enough to be hired by Stonzek, and your show ran for two years then closed, and you knew he had three or four new shows the next season, and you called him hoping he might have a spot for you, he would scream over the phone, "Why are you calling me? Don't call me. If I need you, I'll call you!" And hang up. Saul Guzikoff wasn't quite that bad. (More about him later.)

Fiorello! eventually closed, so it was back to the jungle again!

I started doing dates with the Richard Maltby Orchestra where I made a lasting friendship with Joe Lenza, the lead alto player and road manager; in fact, he became a godfather to our second daughter. Other odd jobs included the 82 Club, a female-impersonator club in GreenwichVillage. (A lot of laughs reminding me of my burlesque days.)

One Wednesday afternoon while at the union floor, I met Harry Wuest, who contracted musicians for several road bands, including Buddy Morrow, Bob Crosby, Vaughn Monroe, Sammy Kaye, Tex Beneke, Ray McKinley, Wayne King, Xavier Cugat, and the Billy May band.

I worked with all of them at one time or another that year. (I will have stories about each of them later.)

In the spring of 1964, my friend Joe Lenza recommended me to Paul Lavalle, the conductor of the Band of America, scheduled to work at the New York World's Fair.

I figured it would run through the summer when things were normally very slow. The hours were 11:00 a.m. to 7:00 p.m., six days a week at $175.

We would meet at the band's staging area, board a three-car motorized tram, stop at designated areas around the fairgrounds, and play a twenty-minute concert. Then at six o'clock proceed to the fountain area and give a full-hour concert. (The thing that bothered me the most was having to wear a military band-type hat!)

I have to admit I was not very happy there.

One hot, muggy afternoon, three young rednecks kept following us around the park, yelling, "Play Dixie! Play Dixie!" We ignored them until we pulled in to the fountain area to give our hour concert where they kept braying, "Play Dixie! Play Dixie!"

Paul Lavalle announced over the microphone, "These young men have been requesting all day that we play 'Dixie,' so now we're going to play it for them. He turned toward the band and said, "Get up, Dixie." He seemed to be looking directly at me. Now, when I was on the road with the Spivak band and we played anywhere in the South such as a veterans club, Elks, Moose, or any other fraternal organization, we would always be requested to play "Dixie"; and when we did, they would jump up, turn toward the Confederate flag, and salute! This bugged the shit out of me, so one night when I was drinking, I swore I would never play "Dixie" again! So when Lavalle looked at me, I just sat there with my horn on my lap. He said it again, "Get up, Dixie." I rebelled and just sat there while the band played it.

When we got back to the staging area and I was packing up my horn, one of Lavalle's flunkies said to me, "The maestro would like to see you in his dressing room."

I was all set for some kind of confrontation, so when I got to his room, he was sitting at his table, checking some notes on some music. After a moment, he looked up and said very softly, "Daryl, you aren't very happy here, are you?" His quiet demeanor kind of took the wind out of my sail, so I said, "No, Paul, I'm not." "Well," he said, "this probably isn't the kind of job you are used to, so if you feel you'd rather not come back tomorrow, it'll be all right." I just said, "Okay" and left.

After the world's fair, I landed three more Broadway shows. *Skyscraper* starring Julie Harris, *Mr. President* with Robert Ryan and Nanette Fabray, and *All American* starring Ray Bolger, none of which lasted more than a few months.

I believe it was about this time that the seeds of discontent about living and working in New York were sown.

CHAPTER SIXTEEN

The King of Swing

In the spring of 1965, a surprising phone call came in one afternoon from Jay Fiengold, Benny Goodman's manager. He said that Benny was putting a new band together for a two-week engagement at Freedomland, a quasi-amusement park in the Bronx, and could I come to a rehearsal at Nola Studio about two o'clock the next afternoon.

When I got there, the band was already playing, and there were several other trumpet players waiting to sit in, some I knew, some I didn't. Benny kept switching them around to different chairs while rehearsing. Finally, he looked at me and said, "Flea, take the first chair." I was surprised that he knew my name.

I had grown up listening to the Benny Goodman band and loved that style, so it was a great kick for me to play those arrangements that I had heard so many times on records.

We played about three tunes then Benny said, "That's it, fellas, thanks for coming." While I was packing up my horn, Jay Feingold came over and said, "Benny says you're hired, I'll call you in a couple days with the details."

I know there are dozens of stories about Benny Goodman, but here's one of my own.

About the third afternoon at Freedomland, we were doing a local broadcast, and there were about five hundred people crowded around the stage. The local announcer had just introduced the band and said, "Now Benny and the boys start off with an old favorite, 'Love for Sale.' Take it away, Benny!"

Benny was standing in front of the band, his back to the audience, humming the tune and scratching his ass! We kept waiting for the count off; you couldn't take your eyes off him because it could come at any time, and you had to be ready.

Gene Allen, the baritone saxophone player, started to laugh. Benny saw him and said, "Hey, Pops, what's so funny?" Gene was a little embarrassed and said, "Oh, nothin', Benny, I'm ready." Benny continued, "No, Pops, let us all know what's so funny."

Gene was squirming. "Nothin', Benny, nothin'." Benny said, "I'll tell you what. Why don't you take your axe (saxophone) and go down there and laugh," pointing to the crowd. Gene picked up his horn and walked off the bandstand. Now the bass player is laughing! Benny saw him and said, "Hey, Pops! Why don't you go down and join him?" We finished the broadcast without the baritone saxophone or bass.

The other trumpet players at that time were George Triffon, Harold Lieberman, and the legendary Cootie Williams. (One reviewer wrote it was the first time he had ever seen a cootie and a flea in the same trumpet section!) Another fine player, Jimmy Nottingham, joined us the second week. (When I sat between Cootie and Jimmy, both black, they called me Oreo!)

At the end of the Freedomland engagement, Jay Feingold said that Benny had a tour coming up in about a month, ending in California at Disneyland and that he wanted me to do it. I told Jay that I had been recommended to do a new Broadway show, and I was afraid that if I was out of town when the call came, I might not get it. The show I was referring to was *Jenny* starring Mary Martin. This was the one that Johnny Lesko had told me about months earlier. Johnny didn't get the job as conductor, but he would be the piano player and assistant conductor, and he had recommended me to the contractor Saul Guzikoff.

I couldn't believe it when my phone rang one evening, and Benny Goodman was on the other end of the line. "Hey, Pops, Jay says you don't want to go to the West Coast with me."

"No, Benny, that's not it." I told him about the show and said I was afraid if I wasn't in town—if the call came in and I wasn't here, I could lose out. He said, "Who's the contractor?" I told him Saul Guzikoff. He said, "You'll hear from him tomorrow." I said, "Benny, if you do that for me, I'll make the tour whether I get the show or not, thank you."

Sure enough the next day, Guzikoff called. "Boy, you have a good friend. Benny Goodman called and said I should use you in my new show, but Jay Blackton is the conductor, and you have to audition for him." I figured, *Okay, what the hell.* He said, "Be at Jay's apartment tomorrow evening at seven o'clock with your horn." I was a little early (I'm a Virgo), and while I was getting my horn out of the case, Blackton set up a little wire music stand in the middle of his living room with the first trumpet part to the overture of "Guys and Dolls" on it. He stood in front of me with his baton and started to conduct. Saul Guzikoff was sitting in a corner reading the newspaper. When he finished, Blackton turned to Saul and said, "Well, you finally brought me someone who can follow the stick." I said to myself, *Man, I'm in!* Blackton thanked me and said Guzikoff would be in touch. The next day Guzikoff called and offered me the show on third trumpet! (Oh well!)

I called Jay Feingold and told him to tell Benny that I would do the tour. Our first stop was at Ravinia, an outdoor amphitheater outside of Chicago. They put us up in cabins on the grounds and sent limos to pick us up and take us to the stage. It was an early-evening concert, so there was a lot of daylight left. One limo picked three of us up at our cabin then went to the next cabin to pick up Cootie Williams. Cootie sat in the front seat, mumbling and appearing agitated. I said, "Cootie, what's the matter?" He turned around and said, "Man, we in the country. I can't play no jazz in the country. I gots to be downtown where the bright lights and the pretty girls is!"

I found out later that over seven thousand people were at that concert!

The tour continued also stopping at the Air Force Academy outside of Denver, Colorado, and then onto California and Disneyland.

Working for Benny Goodman could be trying. He was a very erratic man. You never know when it might be your day in the barrel and that you might be singled out and, for some unknown reason, become the object of his displeasure. Thankfully, it never happened to me, but I witnessed it with other guys. Nevertheless, I'm glad that I had the opportunity to play with that band!

To add a postscript to this chapter, in the fall of 1963, we started rehearsals for the show *Jenny*. It looked like a winner. Mary Martin, direction by Josh Logan, how could we lose? We found out on opening night when during the lukewarm applause for Mary Martin's curtain call, someone in the balcony called out, "Better luck next time, Mary!" The show ran for sixty performances, just enough to cover the advance sale. (We did do a cast album, which you can now buy on eBay for $4.99.)

CHAPTER SEVENTEEN

Moon over Miami

The next few years brought several changes. For one, we sold our $23,000 house in Queens for $24,000 and bought a brand-new two-story, three-bedroom home in Manhasset Hills in Nassau County for $39,900. (Which Lynn sold twenty-two years later for $362,000!)

The commute to Manhattan was via the Long Island Expressway, which later became known as the world's longest parking lot! Ordinarily, it should take no more than thirty to forty minutes to midtown, but that was not always the case. Parking at night in Manhattan became impossible. To get to midtown, I had to drive to Long Island City, try to park near a subway stop, and take the train the rest of the way. After work, it was a train back to Long Island City, rush to my car, hoping not to get mugged, and drive home.

The one bright spot was the birth of our third child. Our daughter Juda Lynn was born on April 3, 1966.

Lynn was doing very well with her jingle dates while I kept fairly busy doing whatever came along. I subbed in several Broadway shows, did a brief stint with the house band at the new Americana Hotel on the corner of Forty-ninth Street and Seventh Avenue where drummer Sol Gubin remarked, "This is a nice hotel, but it's too far from the beach!"

I recorded two albums with the Buddy Morrow band plus some weekend dates.

Chuck Goldstein made me the contractor for his jingle company if the jingle date called for musicians, which was great because I got to hire the best musicians in New York, but even with that, somehow, I was not content.

The uncertainty of the music business started me thinking that maybe I should try something else, possibly photography, so I spent a week knocking on doors of photo studios in Manhattan, offering to work cheap just to get some experience. How naïve, even when I offered to work for nothing, no one was interested.

I answered an ad in the local Long Island newspaper for a photographer's assistant. The guy that ran the ad was a local photographer who worked out of his house doing weddings, school photos, etc.

When I went to his home for the interview, the strangest thing happened. While we were talking, I kept hearing this music in the background that I recognized. It was recordings of the Jimmy Lunceford Orchestra! It seems he loved Jimmy Lunceford. When he found out I was a musician and could name every guy in the Lunceford band, the interview was over, and I was hired.

I soon found out, however, that he was not a very good photographer. He took me with him on a few jobs, loading film, setting up lights, and during the school photo sessions, trying to keep the hostile little bastards sit still and smile. (Ha!)

The end came one day when we returned to the house after taking fifty or sixty graduation pictures. My job was to take the rolls of film to the darkroom and, in total darkness, clip them to a wire and lower them into a deep tank of developer. Somehow, I failed to attach the film securely to the clips, so when I went to retrieve it, all the clips were empty! My heart sank! A whole day's work possibly ruined. I plunged both arms deep into the developer, fished around for the film lying on the bottom, then rushed it to the trays of fixer.

When I came out of the darkroom, soaked in developer, my shirt ruined, the guy I worked for wanted to know what had happened. When I tried to explain, he went berserk! How could I be so stupid, ruining the whole day's worth of film? (Actually, the film wasn't ruined, just a little overdeveloped.)

He wouldn't let up, bitching and chastising me the rest of the day. I left and never went back. Maybe the music business wasn't so bad after all.

After the holidays, that winter, I told Lynn that I needed to get away from New York for a while and wanted to try my luck in Florida. She said she understood; I believe she thought a short time away might help me get what was bothering me out of my system.

Lynn was doing three or four jingle dates a week, so we hired a nanny, a nice lady from Central America to help with the children when we were both working. I called a trumpet-player friend of mine, Jimmy Longo, who was now living in Miami Beach, and asked if he could put me up for a while. He said, "Sure, if you don't mind sleeping on a cot."

I drove to Miami and, a few days later, received a call from the contractor at the Fontainebleau Hotel, saying that I had been recommended by my friend Paul Cohen to do five weeks at the hotel with Frank Sinatra.

Sinatra was also shooting the movie *Lady in Cement* in Miami at that same time.

I must say that five-week engagement stands out as one of the musical highlights of my career!

The orchestra was excellent, just one show a night, great arrangements, and Sinatra seemed pleased the whole time. He even used the orchestra to record a commercial he was doing for Caesar's Palace in Las Vegas.

About that recording session: the sound guys at the studio set the band up with each section in a circle with a microphone in the center. Sinatra walked in, took one look at the setup, and said, "All wrong! Set this up like a big band, saxes in front, trombones behind them, and trumpets on a riser behind the trombones, piano, bass, and drums together on the side!"

The commercial was a swinging arrangement by Billy May. We ran it down a couple of times then went for the first take.

At the end of the third take, which was perfect, there was silence from the control booth. Sinatra asked, "Well?" From the booth the sound engineer said, "That was great, Frank, we want to do one more." Sinatra answered, "If it was great, you don't need another one!" He turned and waved to the band, "Thanks, fellas." and walked out.

The night before closing, while the curtain was closed, Frank came out and said to the orchestra, "This has been a great gig, so tomorrow night, you are all invited after the show to a party in the Poodle Lounge (a famous watering hole in Miami.) Bring your wife, your broad, or both, if you want to!"

The next night after the show, we all headed for the Poodle Lounge. Sinatra's bodyguards were at the door, making sure no one got in except members of the orchestra. The bar was open, and a buffet was set up with all kinds of wonderful food.

I thought this was very generous of Sinatra, but I really didn't expect him to be there. But to my surprise, in he came with three of the stars of his new movie. Richard Conte, Raquel Welch, and the comedian B.S. Pulley!

They went to the bar; Frank ordered a drink then excused himself and went to each table, shook hands with each member of the orchestra, complimented the wife or girlfriend, and said, "Eat, drink, and stay as long as you want."

I had the privilege of working with Frank Sinatra several times after I moved to California. I have a beautiful colored, autographed photograph of Frank that I framed myself, along with a gold Saint Christopher medal that he gave to all of us in the Les Brown band, with a card that reads, "With my love and affection, Francis Albert." (That's class!)

The Miami local had given me a union card because of the Sinatra engagement, so I decided to stay in Florida a little longer. I did several shows at the Deauville Hotel through the spring. Summer in Miami is pretty slow, work wise, plus I was feeling a little guilty about being away from my family so long, so I said good-bye to the palm trees and headed back to New York.

The next winter found me once again heading south. My friend Dr. Joe Groom invited me to stay at his home in Coral Gables and help him with an airplane he was building. He wanted me to do the woodwork on the rudder, elevators, and wing ribs. He had another guy do the welding on the fuselage using aircraft metal tubing, and that required special skill.

It was an open-cockpit, two-seater biplane called Starduster Two. I left Florida before it was finished, but I got to ride in it a year later, flying over the Florida Keys with the leather helmet, goggles, and scarf, just like John Wayne in the movie *Flying Leathernecks*!

My unrest and trips away from home began to take a toll on the relationship with my wife. I knew that my responsibility was to be with my family, so I vowed to stay put and make the best of it.

Back in New York, I got a call to record a soundtrack on a new Woody Allen movie. It was a two-day session in a studio on West Forty-second Street in Manhattan at 10:00 a.m. I left my house at eight fifteen, figuring I had plenty of time to get to the date.

At 10:00 a.m., I was sitting in my car in the middle of the Fifty-ninth Street Bridge, pounding the steering wheel in frustration. When I finally got off the bridge, I tore down Second Avenue to Forty-second Street, left my car in a no-parking zone, and rushed up the stairs to the studio. Bernie Glow and Mel Davis were in the foyer of the studio. When they saw me, they said, "Take it easy! They haven't gotten to us yet." That experience with New York traffic helped push me toward the decision that I made a few months later.

During that recording session, Mel Davis asked me if I was busy the following Thursday. I said, "No, why?"

He said he had a double-record date that day, and could I sub for him on *The Tonight Show*.

To be on staff at NBC, CBS, or ABC was as good as it got in New York and especially to be in *The Tonight Show* band. Milton Delugg was the leader; and the trumpet section included Mel Davis, Jimmy Maxwell, and Dick Perry.

Rehearsals for *The Tonight Show* started at four o'clock for an hour or so, depending on how much music the band had to play, then broke until seven o'clock when the taping started. (Most people thought they were watching the show live at eleven o'clock.)

For the next three months, I subbed at least two or three days a week for Mel, Jimmy, or Dick. Then the curtain fell!

I don't remember why, but one night, Johnny Carson walked off the show. When he returned, after negotiations with NBC, one of the stipulations was that he could bring in Doc Severinsen, his own bandleader.

When Doc took over the band, he brought in Johnny Frosk, my friend from the Dorsey band, and Clark Terry. He also ruled no outside subs! (It sure was fun while it lasted.)

Soon *The Tonight Show* moved to California, and eventually all the staff jobs in New York were gone. There is no such thing as a staff orchestra in this country now.

After the brief time with *The Tonight Show* band, I started working weekends again for Harry Wuest with pickup bands he put together. He told me Sammy Kaye had two weeks at Disneyland in Anaheim, California, and that if I was willing to drive out there, I could work three or four one-nighters on the way with Bob Crosby. I came up with a great idea! My son had just turned eight and was out of school for summer vacation. What a wonderful time to make a cross-country trip, just the two of us, so we packed up the station wagon and headed West!

We picked up Bob Crosby somewhere in Pennsylvania, played a gig there, then one in Ohio and one in Wisconsin. We continued our trip through Illinois, Missouri, and then into Oklahoma where we came upon a huge trading post selling all kinds of Western goodies! We spent two hours looking at Indian jewelry, Texas longhorn wall plaques, and cowboy memorabilia. I said to my son, "Let's wait until we get further west. I think we might find more authentic items and better prices." (Actually, I was wrong. We didn't see anything better or cheaper all the way to California.)

We had fun collecting decals from every state we passed through. My son would stick them on the rear-side window of the station wagon. By the time we got home, both windows were covered.

We spent two days taking in the Grand Canyon in Arizona, which was great, and then on to Anaheim and Disneyland.

At the end of the two weeks, we packed up the station wagon and headed for home. Bob Crosby had invited us to visit him at his home in La Jolla, so we stopped there and played a round of golf at his country club.

I decided to go through Reno, Nevada, and visit with Sam Donahue, my friend from the Dorsey band who was now leading a band at one of the casinos in Reno.

Since we hadn't seen any souvenirs as nice as the ones at the trading post in Oklahoma, we decided to retrace our steps and stopped at that trading post on our way home. It was really a wonderful trip, and I know both my son and I will never forget it.

Now back in New York, I was scuffling for the rest of the summer, doing a few dates for Harry Wuest, then a couple of weeks at Freedomland with Johnny Long and Richard Maltby.

Lynn and I seemed to be drifting farther apart, so when Harry Wuest told me he was moving to West Palm Beach, and if I wanted to go there he could keep me busy through the fall and winter, I agreed. He was contracting all the shows that would be coming to the convention center such as Holiday on Ice, the Lipizzan Stallions, and Ringling Brothers Circus, plus all the road bands he was handling.

Lynn was doing great in the jingle business, and I knew I couldn't ask her to give that up and move to Florida, nor would I; but I was unhappy, and she seemed to understand. We both agreed to separate for a while.

I packed up my station wagon and hit the New Jersey Turnpike, headed south, never to again live in New York.

I arrived in West Palm Beach and bought a single wide mobile home for $4,500 in the same mobile-home park that Harry Wuest had moved into. It was on a nine-hole golf course, and the lot rent was $63 a month! This is where the fun starts!

CHAPTER EIGHTEEN

A Medley of Bob Crosby, Xavier Cugat, Liberace, Vaughn Monroe, Wayne King

I had just moved into my mobile home in West Palm Beach when I got a call from Harry Wuest about doing a week with Bob Crosby on the island of Jamaica for the Tappan Gas Range Co. at their annual convention.

It was to be a six-piece band—I on trumpet, Buddy Morrow on trombone, a piano player and bass player from West Palm Beach, and the Jamaica musicians' union insisted that we use two Jamaican musicians! Harry said we only had to do two shows, and we would be staying at the Jamaica Hilton Hotel. Sounded great!

We flew over to the island, got on an old rickety bus, and proceeded to the hotel.

The Jamaica Hilton was smack-dab in the middle of the jungle! The nearest little town was a $12 cab drive each way!

Rehearsal was set for eleven o'clock, and we were all there except the Jamaican musicians. Some tall Jamaican native said he was the manager of the musicians we were waiting for. He said in a thick Jamaican accent, "Don't worry, mon, dey will be here, dey live on the other side of the mountain." They finally showed up at three o'clock. A drummer and a saxophone player. I knew we had a problem when I saw palm trees painted on the bass drum and cymbals that looked like old tin pie plates. The saxophone player was an ex-French foreign legion soldier. He had an old silver saxophone with the mouthpiece so corroded that he couldn't move it to tune up. (Not that it mattered, he couldn't play it anyway!) Crosby told him to just sit there and look as though he were playing.

We got through the rehearsal, playing a couple of Dixieland tunes, and Crosby sang a couple of old standards. I also told Crosby, "You better tell a lot of jokes." He actually was a very good master of ceremonies. He could tell anecdotes about his brother Bing, being Catholic, and golf jokes.

We did about an hour's show that night, and in the middle of it, the power went out, killing the bass amplifier and electric keyboard! When the power came back on, someone in the audience hollered out, "Play 'Night Train,'" which had been a hit record for Buddy Morrow, recorded with a sixteen-piece band. Buddy looked at me, I looked at him, we both looked at Crosby, and Buddy said, "What the hell, let's do it!"

Fortunately, the bass player and piano player knew the song, and we told the drummer, "Just hit the drum on two and four." And off we went, one trumpet, one trombone, playing a sixteen-piece arrangement of "Night Train"!

We finished to a standing ovation! Unbelievable! Buddy and I still laugh about it today.

Buddy had just married his girl singer, Carol (still his wife), so this trip to Jamaica was to be their honeymoon. We figured for the next few days we would just lie around the pool and soak up some sun, but the next morning, one of the conventioneers had a heart attack in the pool and drowned! The local police shut down the pool to investigate, which lasted for the rest of the week. (So much for a nice suntan!) We did our final show and said good-bye to the tropical isle of Jamaica.

My next Crosby story took place a little later that year in December. We had four or five dates around North Florida and Georgia with another Harry Wuest pickup band. Crosby rode with me and the equipment, music stands, music case, etc.

We checked into a motel outside of some small town where we were to play at the local country club. We had passed a steak house about five miles back on the highway, so Crosby said, "Let's go back to that steak house for dinner."

We were about halfway back to the motel after dinner when suddenly Crosby said, "Oh boy, hurry up, I have to get to the bathroom fast!" When I stopped at his room, he jumped out of the car and rushed like a madman for the door. I called to him, "I'll pick you up at eight o'clock."

At eight o'clock, I knocked on his door, no answer. I knocked again, and the door swung open a few inches, it wasn't locked. I called, "Bob?" No answer. I pushed the door open and called again, "Bob?"

You have to imagine this scene. I looked to the left, and in the corner of the room was a large television set with a beautiful colored picture of brother Bing singing "White Christmas," and to my right, on his hands and knees in the bathroom, was brother Bob wiping up the remains of the diarrhea that had let loose before he reached the toilet! I looked at the picture of Bing then at Bob and thought, *Why this one?*

He came out of the bathroom, white as a sheet, with a bath towel wrapped around his waist. I noticed his legs looked all scratched up. I said, "What happened?" He told me he had taken his soiled underwear, wrapped it in a towel, gone out behind the motel in the dark, and threw it into the weeds. Then he remembered his name was embroidered on the waistband, and he was afraid someone would find it, so in the dark, he fumbled around in the weeds and brambles but never did retrieve it.

I had many conversations with Bob and always had the feeling that he felt his brother Bing should have done more to help him along. I couldn't understand why he felt that way because he was a good entertainer in his own right. Not as good a singer as Bing, but he had a successful band, made recordings, and had his own daytime television show for a while; but I guess it wasn't easy being Crosby number 2.

The next call from Harry Wuest was about a seven-day cruise to, of all places, Jamaica with Xavier Cugat. A rehearsal was called for the night before we were to leave. Another pickup group! Three saxes, two trumpets, one trombone, bass, drums, and piano. Cugat carried with him a Mexican singer, a conga drum player, and his no-talent wife Charo! (She walked around carrying her little Chihuahua, ignoring the guys in the band and berating Cugat constantly.)

I didn't know anyone in the band except Stan Edson, the tenor player. Most of them were pretty young, especially the Fender bass player and the drummer who had acne.

Cugat called up the first arrangement, a rhumba, and beat it off. After four bars, he stopped the band. The drummer wasn't playing. It seemed he hadn't a clue about how to play a Latin tempo! Cugat was furious! He threw his hands up in the air and walked around, screaming, "I'm Cugie, I'm Cugie, what will people think if I can't play my music?" Of course, Harry Wuest was nowhere to be found, and it was too late to try to replace the drummer, so I tried to console Cugat and said I would work with the drummer and show him how to play a Latin beat. There was nothing else we could do.

I was acting road manager, so we packed my station wagon with the equipment, including a large wooden case about the size of a coffin that belonged to the conga player. I wondered what the hell was in there. I soon found out. It seemed he carried a shrine with him to the Virgin Mother. He shared a stateroom with the Mexican singer, so he put the shrine between the two beds. He placed a banana and an apple on the shrine as an offering to the saint.

When the Mexican singer showed up and saw the fruit, he ate it. This flipped out the conga player, so he put a curse on the Mexican singer!

We opened the show that night and somehow got through the first number. Cugat introduced the Mexican singer, and we went into the introduction of his first song, "La Cucaracha." Out he came, dressed in an all-white Mexican outfit with a big white sombrero and two pearl-handled revolvers. He went way out to the front of the dance floor, which was quite a distance from the bandstand. He apparently couldn't hear the band or the tempo (because the kid drummer was screwing it all up), so he turned toward the band, waving his arms, and hollered something in Spanish. Cugat began to holler back, "Sing, just sing!" The Mexican wouldn't give up, he kept shouting in Spanish at Cugat. Finally, Cugat waved at him and hollered, "Get off the stage, you're fired! Get off!" I took a quick look at the conga player. He was smiling!

The first time I worked with Vaughn Monroe was at the famous Rainbow Room atop Rockefeller Center in New York City. It was a small eight-piece band, and we just played for dancing.

One night, near the end of the job, Vaughn turned to the piano player and said, "Give me an arpeggio into the verse of 'I Wish You Love.'" He started to sing. "Good-bye, no use leading with our chins, this is where the story ends, no use leading with our chins. Good-bye, this is where the story ends, no use leading with our chins, this is where the story ends," he sang the whole sixteen-bar verse with just two lines! I wasn't sure I'd heard it correctly, so I looked up at him. He was bombed! Vaughn was a tall distinguished, good-looking man, who, as I learned later, could hold his liquor pretty well up to a point!

A month or so later, Harry Wuest sent me out with Vaughn on about ten days of one-nighters. The first date was at the Club outside of Birmingham, Alabama, a place I have mentioned in a previous chapter, having worked it with Tommy Dorsey.

We got to the job early, and Vaughn asked me to come to his dressing room. He said they wanted an hour's show before the dance, so what should we do? I thought, *What should we do? What should you do? You're the leader!*

This was another Harry Wuest pickup band, most of whom I didn't know and were quite young. The first saxophone player had hair that reached halfway down his back!

I went through Vaughn's library and tried to pick out things that would work as a show. He had had some hit records "Racing with the Moon," "Dance Ballerina Dance," "Ghost Riders in the Sky," and "There I Said It Again." We certainly had to do those! I also told him to think of some jokes!

Somehow we got through the show okay then started to play dance music. I noticed a table of about four rednecks seated near the bandstand. They were drinking beer and soon were pointing at the long-haired saxophone player and using their fingers like scissors as though they were going to cut off his hair! I was glad when that night ended.

Two or three times, during the remaining one-nighters, Vaughn would get so loaded by the end of the job that I would have to prop him up in a doorway and tell him to stay put until I got the car. Little old ladies would be trying to talk to him, to tell him how wonderful they thought he was, but all he could do was stare glassy-eyed and mumble incoherently!

He was really a nice man though and, at the end of the tour, invited the whole band to visit his home in Florida. He had a lovely house in a gated community right on the ocean.

During that time, I lived in West Palm Beach. I did two concert tours with Liberace, probably the most flamboyant entertainer I had ever worked with. We played mostly convention centers and huge concert halls, and when the venue permitted, he would make his entrance onstage in a chauffeur-driven Rolls-Royce! He played on a white concert grand piano that traveled with the show wherever we went (And of course the candelabra!), and the show was always sold-out!

Everything was first class—the orchestra, the accommodations—and Liberace treated everyone who worked with him with respect.

He was fun to watch, especially when he would leave the piano and go down into the audience to show all the ladies his jewelry; they went wild!

On one of the tours, he carried about twenty native steel drum players and their steel drums, all shapes and sizes, literally filling the stage. They were great! They would perform difficult compositions such as the "Poet and Peasant" overture.

We played an auditorium in Daytona Beach, and I invited my mother to the show. After the performance, I took her backstage and luckily found the opportunity to introduce her to Liberace. He made a big fuss over her, saying how proud she must be to have such a talented son! He made her feel like Queen for a Day! I must say, Liberace was a real gentleman!

Probably the most unorthodox bandleader I ever worked for was Wayne King, "the Waltz King"! Harry Wuest said Wayne needed a trumpet player that could play the Al Hurt arrangement of "Jada," a big record for Al on his concert tour. I knew Wayne King had a style band out of Chicago, so I thought it might be interesting. Also, an old friend of mine, Bob Magee, a tenor saxophone player that had been on the Spivak band with me, was now playing lead alto with Wayne King, so I thought we might have a few laughs! (Little did I know!)

The first thing McGee said to me was, "You're not going to believe this." I said, "Bob, I've been on a lot of bands, what could be so different?" He just laughed and repeated, "You're not going to believe it."

I learned that Wayne King had his own set of rules. Rule number1: When the bus driver announced over the PA system on the bus that the call is 8:00 a.m., it meant that you were to be in your seat at seven forty-five or you are considered late. Rule number 2: The girl singer Nancy Evans, a very nice lady who lived in Orlando, Florida, sat in the first right-hand seat, and you were not to converse with her at any time. Actually, the bus driver was instructed to escort her from her room to the bus and after the job, escort her back to her room when we arrived at the hotel. (After I moved to Orlando, I had lunch with Nancy several times; but on the second tour I did with Wayne, rule number 2 applied!)

A Wayne King concert was rather strange. The opening number was "Tales from the Vienna Woods," and then it slowed down! After several syrupy waltzes, we hit my big number "Jada," the hot tune of the concert!

Wayne had a weird habit of, suddenly in the middle of a song, picking up his saxophone and starting to play a totally different tune. His regular band members from Chicago knew just what to do and went right along with him.

Other times, he would stop the band, pick up his saxophone, and walk to the microphone. He would show the saxophone to the audience and go into his sermon. "This is it, ladies and gentlemen, the original golden saxophone." Then placing his hand over his heart and say in a choked up voice, "And as long as I have a breath in my body, I'm going to play it for you."

The audience cheered! I finally leaned forward, tapped my friend Bob on the shoulder, and said, "You were right! I don't believe it!"

I worked with several other bandleaders during this period, including Tex Beneke, a good guy who felt more comfortable being a sideman than a leader.

Ray McKinley was leading the Glenn Miller band. I did quite a few dates and a cruise with Ray. We got along great because we both were fans of W. C. Fields and spent a lot of time imitating him (more about Ray in the next chapter).

CHAPTER NINETEEN

Top of the World

Late in 1970, it had become known that the Disney Corporation had been secretly buying up twenty-five thousand acres west of Orlando, Florida.

Rumors started flying that they would be hiring musicians, but no one knew who would be in charge or in what capacity they would be used.

One day, Harry Wuest told me that one of the large hotels to be built on Disney property would be the Contemporary Resort and would have a restaurant and showroom on the top floor called the Top of the World with about a twelve-piece orchestra to play for the headliners who were scheduled to appear there every two weeks.

Harry confided in me that Ray McKinley was being considered as the leader, and the fact that he had been the contractor for Ray, there was a likely possibility that he would be involved. This was all very hush-hush at the time!

Then one day, he told me that auditions were being held in Orlando and would I like to go with him and help choose brass players for the Top of the World orchestra. He also assured me that I could have the lead trumpet chair and be assistant conductor if I wanted it.

I don't remember too much about those auditions, except that Ray McKinley was there but didn't seem to have much to say about anything.

When we returned to Orlando, Harry told me that McKinley was out and that he, Harry, was now the leader of the orchestra. (I still don't know how that all came about!)

During the next few months, the personnel of the band was set. The saxophone section included Sam Marowitz, from the Woody Herman band, on first alto. Stan Edson, who had been with me on the Cugat fiasco, on jazz tenor; Artie Femanella on second alto; and Dean Kincaid, the great arranger that had written the original Tommy Dorsey's "Boogie Woogie," on tenor and baritone.

I believe we started with two trombones: Paul Voltair, an ex-sergeant major with the West Point Academy band; and Jimmy Foy, who had recently moved to Orlando.

In the rhythm section was Fred Bauwal, who had been with Buddy Morrow's band, an excellent bass player; Gene Traxler, who had been on staff at ABC in New York before all the staff orchestras were dissolved; and one of the best big band drummers in the business, Don Lamond. Marowitz, Traxler, Kincaid, and Lamond all moved to Orlando and bought homes.

Harry asked me if I would be comfortable with Benny Clement on the jazz trumpet chair. Benny and I had worked together on the Liberace and Roger Williams tours and were good friends, so it was fine with me.

Also, Bob Cross, who had been the bandleader at the Shoreham Hotel in Washington DC and was now director of entertainment at Disney World, asked if we could find a spot for his first trumpet player, Billy Spano. I knew Billy was a strong player and could help with relief lead if necessary, so I said, "He'll be fine!"

We were told that the opening was scheduled for October 1971, so Harry and I decided to move to Orlando that summer. I put my mobile home up for sale and sold it soon for $5,000, a $500 profit!

Orlando wasn't a very big town, so there wasn't much to choose from as far as rental apartments were concerned. We found a nice complex called Spanish Trace, but it was in Altamont Springs, about twenty-five miles from Disney.

The deal was we would be working at Disney World, that we would not be Disney employees but independent contractors, consequently not subject to all the restrictive and punitive rules endured by Disney employees such as no facial hair, collar-length haircuts, etc! (I could keep my Van Dyke!)

Disney did provide us with very nice lightweight semiformal outfits that fit in with the decor of the nightclub restaurant.

We opened in October as scheduled, and I believe the first act that we played for was Patti Page.

For the first month, we shared a dressing room with a mariachi band that played at different locations around the Contemporary Resort. Later they found an empty room for us, two floors below the restaurant, gave us some lockers and a couple of tables and chairs.

It was rather an easy job. The hours were seven thirty to twelve. That included two fifty-minute shows, three short dance sets, and a forty-five-minute break after the first show to allow them to prepare for the second seating (and also allowed us to go downstairs to the employee's cafeteria where I got my sugar fix for the day in the form of a piece of great chocolate cake à la mode for $0.60).

We worked six nights a week plus an afternoon rehearsal every two weeks for the new act.

For the first three years, it was wonderful! What could be better? Being able to live in Florida, play with a good band, and make $315 a week!

We played for some great entertainers such as Mel Torme, Jack Jones, Sarah Vaughn, and Barbara McNair. Also comedians like George Kirby and Mimi Hines.

A funny story about Mimi Hines.

Rehearsal was to start at two o'clock, and by two twenty, Mimi still hadn't arrived. When she finally got there at three, she told us what happened.

She was on her way to rehearsal when one of Disney's Gestapo guards noticed that she had a patch sewn on the rear of her blue jeans that said, "Kiss My Patch!" which was a no-no, so they made her go back to her room and change.

The club did great business. There was a minimum charge for each show, and the place was usually sold-out. It seemed as though anything Disney touched turned to gold, no matter how dumb some of the things they did. For instance, they had a great maître d', a Cuban gentleman who really knew his stuff. He would escort the customers to their table, keep the waiters and busboys hopping and efficient. If he saw a wineglass empty, he would be there to pour. But then after three months, they replaced him with a young trainee who not only knew nothing about being a headwaiter but wore a tuxedo that didn't fit!

Arnold Palmer, the great golfer who lived in Orlando, frequently came up to the Top of the World to dance and see the shows. Sometimes he would bring his daughter with him and would always come to the bandstand, say hello, and compliment the music.

Mr. Palmer built a beautiful golf course, Bay Hill, outside of Orlando and became very active in the local community.

One night, the Orlando Chamber of Commerce honored Mr. Palmer with the Man of the Year banquet downstairs in the main ballroom of the Contemporary Resort.

I happened to be standing at the entrance of the club, next to the reception podium that night before our second show when the phone on the desk rang.

The little eighteen-year-old girl receptionist answered it, "Hello! Who is this? Mr. Palmer? You want a booth for two for our second show? Can you be here in ten minutes? No? I'm sorry, sir, but we can't seat you once the show starts."

I asked the youngster, "Was that Arnold Palmer?" "I think that was his name," she said. "Do you know who he is?" I asked. The blank look on her face told me she hadn't a clue. Arnold Palmer never came back to the Top of the World again!

During that first year, I met a very attractive German girl and entered into a sometimes-tenuous relationship that lasted for the next seven years, although now, thirty years later, we are still close friends! (My divorce from Lynn had become final that year.)

Disney opened a great little jazz club in the Disney Village, and the first jazz artists to play there were Bobby Hackett backed by the house trio that included my friend Louise Davis, a very good bass player. My lady friend and I went there almost every night after I finished work to hear Bobby.

Quite often, I would drive Bobby back to his condo after work at the jazz club, and he would invite me in for coffee or tea. (We were both AAs.)

We became good friends. A friendship I still cherish.

I got to hang out with some other good friends of mine whenever they played the jazz club. Clark Terry, Urbie Green, and Louis Bellson to name a few.

During my second year at Disney, my mother, who lived in Daytona Beach, passed away. When her affairs were settled and the condo she lived in was sold, the remaining $21,000 was divided equally between my two brothers and myself.

My friend Benny Clement had found a brand-new apartment complex off Orange Blossom Trail, which was twelve miles closer to Disney, so I leased a one-bedroom furnished apartment on a month-to-month basis and moved in.

The area around Orlando was now exploding with new construction. Condo complexes were springing up everywhere. I went to look at one called Tymber Skan, not far from my apartment.

These were one- to four-bedroom condos that featured cedar-plank siding and very rustic looking; curious, I decided to check prices.

I discovered I could buy a one-bedroom condo on a small lake for $16,000 with a 10 percent or $1,600 down payment. My mortgage payment would be no more than the rent I was now paying for an apartment.

Remember I had $7,000 from my mother's estate, so I got this bright idea to maybe do something smart for once in my life. People were flocking to Orlando because of Disney, so why not buy a couple more units (I actually bought three more), live in one, and collect rent from the others. Because I worked at Disney, I had no trouble getting approved for the financing.

Things went fine for the first eight months. Then suddenly there were more condos than people to buy or rent them. Some projects actually went belly-up before they were completed. When one or two of my units became vacant, I had difficulty finding new tenants. Rather than having them stand empty, I was forced to lower rents and accept anyone who had the first month's rent and security. My one bedroom on the lake was now renting for $150 a month, and I had trouble getting that!

I had rented my three-bedroom to one of the Top of the World waiters and his wife, two kids, and two Dalmatians. By the time I got rid of them for nonpayment of rent, I had to replace all the carpeting that had been soiled by the dogs.

The four bedroom was repossessed by the mortgage company because I couldn't make up four months of overdue mortgage payments because the guy with four kids was that far behind in his rent.

As I said before, the first three-plus years at Disney was fine. But then things began to change.

Harry came to work every night, but little by little, his outside interests seemed to become more important than being the bandleader, so soon I was leading the band more and more.

Most of the entertainers brought their own conductors, but on occasion, I would have to take over that duty. I conducted for Bobby Rydell, Helen O'Connell, and one or two others whose names escape me!

Harry would be gone for weeks at a time, and one or two of the guys began to take advantage of the situation. I was the leader, visually, but I had no authority.

On occasion, when I felt the band was getting a little lax musically and offered suggestions to correct it, I was either resented or ignored.

I also became aware that someone in the orchestra, who shall remain nameless, was secretly working to undermine and get rid of Harry Wuest and, eventually, me!

CHAPTER TWENTY

Jukebox Saturday Night

Among Harry's clients were Paula Kelly and the Modernaires, the great vocal group that had been with Glenn Miller, although now, Paula was the only remaining original member.

The group was working as an act. I had played them many times with the Tex Beneke band and other various venues.

In addition to Paula, the group consisted of Tom Traynor, Rich Maxwell, and Vernon Polk, the brother of Gordon Polk, who had been my sponsor in AA.

They all lived in California, but most of their work was on the East Coast. Vernon Polk didn't want to travel anymore, so they asked Harry if he could find someone on the East Coast to work with the group and save them an airfare.

Harry asked me if I would like to join the group since I had had some experience singing with a vocal group when I was with Charlie Spivak.

I already knew most of the lyrics to the Modernaires's tunes, so I called Tom Traynor and asked if he could send me some tapes and the vocal parts to their arrangements, which he did.

The vocal parts weren't complete, so I told Tom that there were a few harmonies I wasn't sure of. His answer was, "Don't worry, Paula can carry it!"

Now I knew that the Paula Kelly of the seventies was not the Paula Kelly of the forties and that she was not the strong lead singer she used to be, so I was rather skeptical of her being able to *carry it*!

The first date we did was in a shopping mall somewhere with a local pickup band and a lousy sound system, but I enjoyed it and thought it might turn out to be fun.

It was for a while. We did several concerts with Ray McKinley and Tex Beneke, and the group really started to sound good. One of the Mod's big hits was "Jukebox Saturday Night," which featured me on a sixteen-bar Harry James-type trumpet solo "Chiribiribin"! (It didn't stop the show, just slowed it down a little!)

Harry booked us into a small club for four days somewhere in Ohio with a house trio that was bugged because they had to read music (our arrangements).

We were supposed to do two shows a night, and we never had more than six people at any one show. It was a miserable four days, plus Paula was juicing, which made everything more uncomfortable.

Our next gig was a ten-day cruise to the Caribbean. We were scheduled to do three shows in the ten-day period, so I suggested to Tom Traynor that we learn some new material and not have to do the same stuff for three shows for the same audience. He agreed and said we could rehearse on the ship.

He scheduled a rehearsal for one o'clock in the afternoon the day of our second show in one of the lounges on an upper deck that had a piano.

He passed out the parts of "Stardust," a beautiful Glenn Miller arrangement they had recorded but hadn't necessarily been a big hit.

Ten minutes into the rehearsal, Paula stopped singing, and in a voice filled with pathos, said, "I just can't do this. I can't be expected to sing all afternoon and then do a show at night." And then she walked out of the rehearsal.

I was furious and directed my anger at Tom Traynor. Of course, he defended her, but my relationship with the Modernaires was damaged permanently!

I was back at the Top of the World when Harry Wuest told me he had just booked the Modernaires for two three-week concerts with Les Brown and the Band of Renown. The premise of the concert was that Les Brown would be featured the first hour, and the second hour would be a tribute to Glenn Miller featuring the Modernaires with Ray Eberle. (Little did I know at that time what a profound change this would make in the direction of my life.)

I had always admired the Les Brown band, so I looked forward to hearing them in person, and I certainly wasn't disappointed. This was how a big band was supposed to sound: great arrangements, a clear, clean ensemble, and a discernible class that I had never noticed in other bands.

The trumpet section included Larry Maguire, Bobby Clarke, Fred Koyen, and Bill Mattison. Les's brother Stumpy held down the bass trombone chair, and in the sax section, on baritone, was Butch Stone, who had already been with Les almost forty years!

Almost every night I would sneak into the audience just to hear the band during their hour of the concert.

Ray Eberle, who had been *Down Beat* magazine's number one male vocalist when he was with Glenn Miller, still sang very well and was also a very nice guy!

He joined us on a couple of the Mod's tunes, just as he had done with the Miller band, and the audience loved it!

Les was also very friendly, and one day during the third week of the tour, we were having lunch together when he asked me if I had ever thought about moving to the West Coast.

I said, "Not really, Les, I wouldn't want to move out there and just be another out-of-work trumpet player."

"No," he said, "I mean to join the band." He took me by surprise.

He continued, "I'm thinking about making a change in the lead trumpet chair, so why don't you think about it."

I did think about it for all of three seconds and said, "I don't have to think about it, Les, I'd love to play with this band."

He asked about giving up my job at Disney World, and I assured him that shouldn't be a problem. We shook hands, and he said, "I'll call you next week so we can talk about it."

Excited, I returned to Orlando but decided not to say anything until everything was all set.

As promised, Les called the following week, but it was not the news I was hoping for.

"The situation has changed, Flea, I had a talk with Larry Maguire, and he said he really needed the job and asked me to reconsider letting him go. So for now, I'm going to leave things just the way they are. Looking forward to seeing you on the next tour."

I was really disappointed, but I said, "I understand, Les. I still have my job here, so no harm done. Thanks anyway. See you on the next tour."

At the end of the first week during the next tour, we were in Atlanta when Les invited me to dinner on a night off.

"Things aren't working out with the lead player, Flea, so if you still want the job, it's yours."

"Yes, I would love to play with the band." I assured him.

"How soon could you be available?" Les asked.

I figured between giving Harry my notice, trying to get rid of the three condos I still had, and driving to Los Angeles would take about four weeks. (This would also mean the end of my relationship with the Modernaires.)

"I can be ready sometime next month," I said. Les shook my hand and said, "Good, we'll work it out. Call Butch when you're ready."

When I got back to Orlando, I called Harry and said I needed to see him. I told him about Les's offer and that I had accepted.

He wished me well and let me know that if things didn't work out, I could always come back to the Top of the World, which I appreciated.

I also told him, as a friend, that I felt that there were forces at work behind his back, trying to sabotage his position at Disney and that he should make more of an effort to take care of business.

Within six months after I left, everything changed at the Top of the World. Harry was out and no more headline acts, instead a new book show called *Kids of the Kingdom*. The band was cut to nine men made to be employees of Disney, and Bob Cross, the entertainment director, became the leader. (The person who was angling for Harry's job remained a sideman!)

CHAPTER TWENTY-ONE

California, Here I Come

The first thing I needed to do was try to get rid of my three condos.

Fortunately, I found a buyer for my two bedroom, the one I was living in, and I asked the Tymber Skan real estate office to do the best they could with the remaining two. (They finally got rid of them for the balance on the mortgage.)

I put the furniture from my condo into storage with a moving company and said I would send for it once I got settled in California.

I called an old friend of mine Tommy King, a trombone player now living in Los Angeles, who had worked with me at radio station WCAE in Pittsburgh and asked him to find me a place to stay temporarily until I could make other arrangements.

I had a Fiat Spyder two-seater convertible, which limited the amount of stuff I could take with me.

I mounted a luggage rack and footlocker on the trunk and packed it with some linens, one plate, one cup and saucer, one knife, one fork, one spoon, one pot, and other assorted sundries!

My Heathkit TV set (I made it myself) sat on the passenger seat, my trumpet bag on the floor of the passenger side, and what clothes I needed were in the well behind the driver's seat!

I stopped to say good-bye to Hildegard, my German lady friend, put the Fiat in gear, and headed West.

Three days later, I stopped somewhere outside of Los Angeles and called my friend to let him know I would be there later that afternoon.

He suggested that I come to his house first, and then he would take me to the place that he had arranged for me, which turned out to be a furnished room over a gas station in north Hollywood.

It really wasn't bad: clean with a single bed, refrigerator, microwave, kitchen table and chairs, and one window that overlooked the garage. The rent: $60 a week!

The best thing though was the restaurant Frank's directly across the street: Greek owned, good food, and reasonably priced. I ate there three times a day and got to know all the waitresses.

I called Butch Stone to let him know I had arrived. He told me to go by Les's office and meet Don Kramer, Les's manager.

Don was very cordial and welcomed me to the band. He took some information from me and gave me the itinerary for the next few weeks.

My first gig with the band was in San Diego at the Hotel del Coronado. A beautiful large all-wooden structure that was once a favorite vacation spot for celebrities. We worked there often over the next several years.

After a couple weeks, Les asked me if I was settled in, and how was I doing.

I said, "Okay, but I wish I had a better place to live." He said, "Why don't you get an apartment?" I said I wanted to, but all my furniture was back in Florida, and I couldn't afford to have it sent out here.

"How much would it cost?" he asked. I told him $2,000.

"Go by the office tomorrow. I'll tell Don to advance you the money. You can pay back a little from each gig until it's settled, okay?"

I found a very nice one-bedroom apartment in a two-family house about six blocks from where I was living now (which meant I could still frequent Frank's restaurant).

When my furniture arrived from Florida, Les's brother Stumpy helped me move it in.

I was very happy about the decision I had made to make the move to California. I loved playing with the band. I'm not quite sure how to explain it, but as I mentioned before, there was a sense of *class* associated with the Les Brown band. Even the name the Band of Renown exemplified it.

At that time, we were working at least three days a week, most of the time high-profile jobs such as movie-studio parties or high-society functions at the Century Plaza Hotel.

We flew to San Francisco at least once a month, or a two- or three-week tour of community concerts across the South or Midwest.

Les paid very well, and when we were out of town, our hotel rooms were paid for plus per diem for meals. Also, Les contributed to the musician's pension fund on every engagement. No other bandleader I ever worked for did that!

The band was also a regular on the Bob Hope television shows of which we did about four a year. Sometimes the show would be broadcast from an out-of-town location such as the Air Force Academy in Colorado, and the band would be included (As long as Hope didn't have to pay for it! Hope's reputation for being frugal was legendary).

I can't attest to the validity of these stories that were told to me by Jeff Clarkson, Hope's piano player, but they fit the image.

It seems Hope was in New York and was scheduled to do an interview at NBC one afternoon. He and Jeff were staying at a hotel just two blocks from the studio. It was raining heavily, so Hope said, "Let's grab a cab." At that time in New York, cab fare was $0.65 for the first quarter of a mile. Being that the studio was just around the corner, that's what showed on the meter.

Hope gave the driver a dollar. When the driver gave him his change, $0.35, Hope gave him a quarter and kept the dime!

One day, Hope received a telephone call from the chairman of a well-known charity, explaining that they were holding a celebrity auction, and if they had an item donated by Bob Hope like maybe a golf bag, it would bring them a sizable amount.

Hope and his secretary climbed the stairs to the second floor of his Toluca Lake estate and opened the door to a room containing three walls lined with golf bags; some still wrapped in plastic that had never been opened.

Hope looked around the room and said, "Hmm! These are very nice!" He turned to his secretary and said, "Send them [the charity] a dozen golf balls!"

At the first Bob Hope television show I did with the band, who should I find in the control booth editing the music but Bob Alberti, the young seventeen-year-old in 1950 who couldn't read music! Bob was now an accomplished composer, arranger, and conductor. We renewed our friendship, which has lasted to this day.

In 1983, we went to Japan on a two-week tour for the Aurex Jazz Festival. With us were Rosemary Clooney, Buddy De Franco, and Georgie Auld. It was a wonderful trip! One day we took the bullet train to Yokohama for an afternoon concert. Art Blakey and the Jazz Messengers were performing on stage before our show.

In his group was a young trumpet player who was beginning to make a name for himself in the music business. His name was Wynton Marsalis. When they finished their set, someone brought him backstage and thought it would be a nice gesture to introduce him to Les's trumpet section. (He wasn't impressed!)

At one time, playing lead trumpet with the Les Brown band could be the ticket into the studios or recording scene, but now that there were no staff orchestras and recording sessions were less frequent, those jobs fell into the hands of a select few.

Then one day, I got a call from my dear friend Sammy Nestico, who was now living in California, telling me that a record company had just signed him to do his own album, and he would like me to play and contract for it. I said to Sam, "Sammy, that's wonderful, but you could get any contractor in Los Angeles to do it."

"I know it," he said. "But I want you to do it. I'll give you a list of the guys I want, no problem, okay?" This is the kind of a friend he is.

The album *Dark Orchid* turned out great! Sammy also recommended me to play on two albums he did for Toni Tennill.

Another friend Vinnie Carbone, who had been Tommy Dorsey's personal manager, recommended me to a record producer from Canada to play, contract, and pick the repertoire of famous trumpet solos for an album starring Al Hirt.

The only recording I got to do with the Les Brown band, thirty instrumentals, was for Muzak. (Commonly referred to as elevator music!)

I have several videos of performances during the time I spent with Les. A concert in Nebraska with Gordon McRae, the jazz festival in Japan, and a PBS show entitled *The Voices of Christmas*.

The show hosted by Mel Tormé featured the band, a wonderful choir, and starred Billy Davis and Marilyn McCoo, impersonator Rich Little, Roy Rogers and the Sons of the Pioneers, George Shearing, Maureen McGovern, and actor Richard Basehart.

Near the end of the show, Richard Basehart was to narrate a beautiful piece of prose entitled "The Stranger," about the life of Jesus Christ. At the dress rehearsal, Les gave the downbeat for the subtone clarinets and the choir to softly play and hum the melody of "Silent Night."

Richard Basehart was seated on a high stool with just a single spotlight overhead. Everyone in the studio was mesmerized by the voice of this fine actor as he began the narration.

Halfway through, he stopped, lowered his head, and was silent. Les stopped the orchestra and choir and waited. Then Mr. Basehart lifted his head, looked directly into the camera, and said, "Aw SHIT, I forgot the next line!"

By 1980, I had turned fifty-six years old and started to feel as though I couldn't play the trumpet forever, so maybe I should prepare myself to do something else. But what?

Looking through the classifieds one day, I saw an ad for a custom picture framing shop for sale for $7,000 in Chatsworth at the western end of the San Fernando Valley. I knew absolutely nothing about picture framing but thought it might be something I would enjoy since I liked working with my hands.

I decided to take a drive out to Chatsworth to look at the shop, but being Sunday, it was closed. I liked the name Masterpiece Frame. I peeked in the window and liked what I saw. I envisioned owning a small business, having a steady income, and not having to worry about how my chops felt on any given day. (Dream on!) I decided to call the next day and make an appointment.

The owner was an older woman whose husband had purchased the business for her just to give her something to do, but now he wanted to move to Colorado and buy a ranch, so she needed to sell. She was firm on the price that included what equipment there was, all the stock, molding, matboard, tools, and the rest, goodwill? I said I could give her $2,000 cash and a note for the rest. She agreed, and we shook hands. She also offered to train me until the sale was finalized.

The so-called equipment was minimal. A mechanical chopper that cut the length and mitered the corners of the molding, ninety-degree-angle devices that held the frame while it was being nailed together by hand, a mat cutter, and assorted hand tools. Really very basic!

Within a year, I had leased to buy a vacuum press, a V-nailer, and a new mat cutter.

Custom picture framing is a low-volume business! For the next seven years, I struggled to keep it afloat. (So much for a steady income!) It was especially hard trying to run the business and still work with the band even though the band gigs were getting less frequent. Both my business and playing suffered. Sometimes there would be a week or more between gigs, and I, not being a practicer (I never had that discipline!), found it difficult to maintain the level of endurance required of a lead trumpet player. So after seven years with the Les Brown band and by mutual agreement between Les and myself, I decided I should leave and devote my energy to, and I quote, "take care of business."

CHAPTER TWENTY-TWO

The Polish Prince

During the second year I was with Les, I was having lunch one day with Vinnie Carbone. He told me he had recently taken over as personal manager for Bobby Vinton, "the Polish Prince."

I knew who Bobby Vinton was, that he had several hit records (none of which I owned), but that was all I knew.

Vinnie said Vinton had just signed a long-term contract to appear at the Riviera Hotel and Casino in Las Vegas two weeks out of every month.

Vinton carried several musicians with him. A young girl piano player and backup singer, a bass player, a trumpet player, and his drummer and conductor, Lloyd Morales.

He had just added a new big band medley to his act in which he played piano, trumpet, clarinet, and alto saxophone. (I use the term *played* loosely!) His trumpet player was a friend from his hometown of Canonsburg, Pennsylvania, who had played with Bobby's father's local band, but now he needed a player with more big band experience. Vinnie told him of my background, so Bobby told him to offer me the job, $600 a week plus my own room at the Riviera Hotel.

It just so happened that Les's band had only one job during that two-week period, so Les said, "Don't worry, we'll get someone to sub for you." For the next two years, I somehow managed to juggle work between Les's band and Vinton.

The Les Brown band worked more than any other big band at that time, but there were periods when things slowed down and one had to take other work if it became available. Les realized that and was very lenient when I needed to take off. Between the two, I was doing okay.

Bobby Vinton was (is) a very good entertainer, and I enjoyed playing his show. He drew big crowds, and his audience loved him.

After Las Vegas, we played Harrah's Casino in Lake Tahoe and then one of the big casinos in Atlantic City, New Jersey.

I had vivid memories of Atlantic City during my basic training in the air corps in 1943 and playing the Steel Pier in the late forties and fifties, but now, sadly, it wasn't quite the same.

Carol, Bobby's twenty-three-year-old piano player and backup singer, and I started hanging out together at the pool every morning in Lake Tahoe. She was from Edgeley, North Dakota, and seemed kinda naïve, but I enjoyed her company, plus she was an excellent piano player. (I couldn't believe a young girl from North Dakota could play such beautiful chord changes!)

As time went on, we began to spend more and more time together until one night . . . !

The apartment I had in North Hollywood was on the second floor, and the elderly couple, not married but living together for convenience, started to complain about my coming home late at night with a lady friend. The stairs to my apartment went right by their front window, so I could see them peeking from behind the curtains, checking on me. I also had a phone answering machine in my hallway that emitted a loud chirp whenever I had a message.

(The old man downstairs informed the landlord that I had some kind of secret electronic machine and that I might be a spy!)

Vinnie called one day and said he had booked Bobby for a one-nighter in Madrid, Spain! It sounded exciting!

We would fly to Madrid, one day for rehearsal, and then do the show the following day.

Apparently, the day before we arrived in Madrid, there had been a political assassination, so when we arrived at the airport, the first thing we saw were soldiers carrying automatic weapons. In fact, they seemed to be on every street corner.

The hotel that we were to stay in can best be described as Spartan! The rooms were very small with bare walls and a small window high up, which made it difficult to look out.

There was a restaurant off the lobby that was open at very different hours than we were used to—breakfast at noon and dinner at 8:00 p.m.

When we arrived for rehearsal, we discovered we would be doing the show in a hockey rink! Wooden planks had been laid on top of the ice to form the stage. There was no heat in the building, and it was freezing!

We got through the rehearsal okay with the local band (no one spoke English). There were three other trumpet players, and they all sounded like Raphael Mendez! They loved playing Bobby's arrangements, and I enjoyed working with them.

We did the show the next evening to an audience of about twenty-five. A real bomb!

Being spring, Carol and I had hoped to spend a few days in southern Spain; but the weather turned sour, chilly, and wet. So we decided against it. On the flight home, twenty minutes before we were to land in New York, Bobby came back to the coach section from his seat in first class and gestured to me to follow him to the flight attendant's alcove. He said he could only take a certain amount of money through customs, so he handed me a fat roll of bills—$9,000—to carry for him. (I guess he didn't care if I got arrested!)

Back in Los Angeles, I found a new apartment, still in North Hollywood, with nice big rooms and a covered garage under the building. It wasn't secured, so a few months later, my little Fiat was stolen. The police apprehended the thieves somewhere outside of Elko, Nevada, so I had to fly there to pick up my car. The convertible top had been slashed, and it was full of empty beer cans and fast-food containers, but no other damage.

Carol had been living in Las Vegas, but she got tired of sin city and decided to move to Los Angeles. A nice one-bedroom apartment became available in my building, so she moved in.

Bobby Vinton was what I like to call a game player. He liked to keep the people that worked for him, guessing. When we would be nearing the end of an engagement, and I wanted to know if he was going to use me on the next one, I would ask Vinnie Carbone.

All Vinnie could say was, "He hasn't decided yet." (Keep 'em guessing!)

Bobby was aware of the situation with Carol and me, so when I asked about the next engagement, Vinnie said Bobby would take me if I agreed to share a room with Carol, presumably saving him the expense of an extra hotel room, which was bullshit because his contract usually provided for hotel rooms! (Plus his hefty fee!)

During his concert, Bobby would introduce his backup people. For instance, he would say, "This is my pianist, Carol." But with his Pittsburgheez pronunciation, it would sound like, "This is my penis, Carol."

Bobby had signed to appear at several other casinos in Las Vegas, so he rented a home off the strip.

A few days before Christmas, he invited his musicians to his home for dinner. For this particular engagement, he had hired a harp player, a rather attractive young lady who took the opportunity to ingratiate herself with the boss by hanging around his dressing room and flirting openly every chance she got, none of which went unnoticed by Bobby's wife, Dolly.

Dolly Vinton had been Bobby's childhood sweetheart. They had been married quite a while and had five children. Dolly could be kind of tough on occasion. If she didn't like you, you probably wouldn't be around very long. Fortunately, she liked Carol very much and even approved of our relationship. (Dolly picked up the tab for my sixtieth birthday party that Carol gave me in Atlantic City.)

Back to the dinner.

We were all seated at his long dinner table enjoying the wonderful food. Bobby and Dolly were seated at one end of the table, and the harp player was at the other end. There was a large basket of hard rolls in front of Bobby, so the harpist, in her cute Marilyn Monroe voice, said, "Bobby, could I have a roll please?"

Dolly, who had had a couple of drinks, picked up a roll and said, "Sure, honey! Here." And with that, she fired the roll the length of the table just missing the blonde curls of the harpist! "In fact, honey, have some more!" Dolly shouted and began throwing rolls one after another, some hitting the mark! The harpist fled, never to be seen again!

I liked Bobby, but sometimes he could be strange.

Case in point:

Vinnie Carbone had been Bobby's personal manager for several years, when one day, while they were having lunch in the Riviera coffee shop, Bobby looked at Vinnie and said, "Vinnie, I've been wondering, just what is it you do for me?" Vinnie looked at him, shocked, and said, "Bobby, if you don't know, then I guess you don't need me!" Vinnie stood up, dropped his napkin on the table, and walked away for the last time.

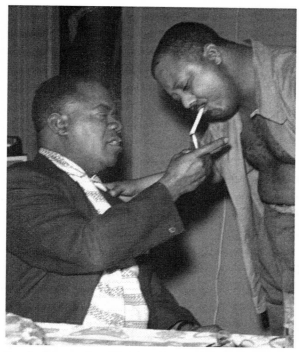

Louis Armstrong, Charlie Shavers, New Years,1957

Dean Martin & Jerry Lewis, last performance
At the Copacobana, Photo by "Flea"

Sammy Kaye, Manhattan Shirt TV Show
Photo by, 'Flea"

Bobby Hackett and Flea, 1972

With Bob Crosby Orch. Disnyland, 1973

Ray McKinley Orch., Cruise ship, 1975

"The Modernairs" 1976
Rich Maxwell, Flea, Paula Kelly, Tom Traynor

Les Brown "Band of Renown" Disnyland, 1979

Les Brown and "Flea"

Bobby Vinton, the "Polish Prince"

Sammy Davis Jr., Frank Sinatra, Dean Martin
Benefit in Hollywood, 1984

My picture framing shop, Chatsworth, Calif.

"Flea and Buddy Morrow, 1992

BAM! Bus accident, Indiana, 1995

Buddy Morrow trpt. Section, Mike Wyatt, Lin Blaisdell, Flea, Bob Carey

Lynn and Flea in Paris

"The Dancing (senior) Campbells"
My 75th. B'day party

Our Kids, Daryl, me, Lynn, Darla, Juda Lynn

Recording session, Lynn, grandson Zachary, Flea, 2005

Zachary Campbell, " Future Star"

"Flea" and Buddy, 2004

Tommy Dorsey Orch w/Budy Morrow, 2007

Friends for fifty eight years!

CHAPTER TWENTY-THREE

The Second Time Around

Carol and I were married in 1981. My dear friend Butch Stone was my best man at our wedding. Les Brown and his wife, Claire, also attended. Carol's parents came from North Dakota and gave us their blessing.

I guess I deluded myself about the age difference not being a problem. It didn't seem to surface the first four years, although I do remember certain times in Las Vegas when, after we would finish our show, I would be content to have a late snack in the coffee shop and then go to our room, whereas Carol would want to go to the lounge to hear some young, contemporary quasi-rock group that for me was too loud and boring.

We gave up our apartments in North Hollywood and moved into a one-bedroom condo in Canoga Park.

Carol was working with Bobby Vinton full-time while I divided my time between the frame shop, Les's band, and Vinton.

After my divorce from Lynn, which was amicable, we stayed in touch, partly because of our three children. I wanted to be part of their lives and because we had remained friends.

Another indication of Carol's youth was that she resented my relationship with the ex-wife. She just couldn't understand it!

Oddly enough, she became good friends with my oldest daughter, Darla. (Just a two-year difference in their ages!)

We stayed in the condo about a year and then decided to buy a place of our own.

Even though we were both working, housing prices being what they were, we could only afford so much.

The real estate lady we were working with suggested we consider a mobile home that was within our price range. She had one listed. A 1,200 square feet, three-bedroom, large kitchen, large family room, living room, and covered carport in Moorpark, just west of Simi Valley. It was rather rural but a nice change from the bustling Central Valley.

The last gig I did with Vinton was a three-week tour of Southeast Asia. We went to Bangkok, Thailand, Hong Kong, and Kuala Lumpur. Some of the shows and places we played were ridiculous, but just being in that part of the world was a wonderful experience.

Back in California, I returned to Les's band and the frame shop until the decision to put the horn away. (I didn't know it would be seven years before I played another note!)

The week after Christmas that year, I took down the Christmas tree and proceeded to haul it through the front door. All the branches had come down, so now it was wider than the doorframe. I pulled and pushed until gradually I finally got it through the opening. I dropped it on the porch and sat down on the step. I was sweating, and a dull pain in my chest caused me some concern.

The next morning, I told Carol I was going to stop by the Kaiser clinic on my way to work and get checked out. (I still had medical coverage from the musicians' union.)

After the examination, the doctor informed me that he suspected that I had experienced a mild heart attack and wanted to put me in the hospital next door for further observation.

After two days, it was determined that I had at least two arteries partially blocked, and that I was a good candidate for angioplasty, a procedure whereby a catheter would be inserted into the artery, and a small balloon would be inflated to open up the artery to facilitate the blood flow. The doctor also prescribed several medications to be taken daily. (Which didn't help my libido any!)

We soon tired of Moorpark and decided to sell the mobile home. We made a small profit and proceeded to buy a new modular home, yet to be built in a new development in Sylmar, just north of the San Fernando Valley.

We picked a lot at the highest elevation in the development, which gave us a wonderful view of the valley.

It took three months for the home to be built, and it was exciting to watch it come together.

The living room had a cathedral ceiling and was large enough to accommodate Carol's baby grand piano.

Carol had been working off and on with Vinton but then quit over a salary dispute.

The frame shop was barely covering expenses, so we needed another income. Carol worked playing piano and singing in the cocktail lounge at several large hotels in Los Angeles, like the Century Plaza, six nights a week for $500. She really didn't like it, but we needed the money, a situation that caused several arguments.

Eventually, Vinton called and asked her to come back at a salary of $1,200 a week.

He had hired a new trumpet player, Cat Anderson, who had been a mainstay of the Duke Ellington Orchestra.

Cat was not a good lead trumpet player, but Bobby was impressed with the screech-high notes Cat was noted for.

One evening, after Carol had come home after a two-week stint in Las Vegas, and while we were having dinner at a Love's barbecue restaurant, Carol confessed to me that she had been having an affair with a saxophone player, arranger, who was also married and had joined Bobby's group.

I never saw it coming and, for the moment, was speechless. During my seventeen-year marriage to Lynn, I never had to deal with the unpleasant problem of infidelity.

My first reaction was shock then hurt then anger! Later that night, after berating the situation for several hours, I told her I needed her to end the affair so that we could try to work out any problems between us. Her answer was "I'm not sure I want to end it."

Being a Virgo, I made what I thought was a practical decision, and by the next day, I had signed a month-to-month lease on a studio apartment with a Murphy bed, five blocks from my frame shop.

After several unsuccessful attempts to reconcile, I accepted the fact that it was over.

Believe it or not, the day I moved, she actually helped me carry several cartons and the clothes I needed into my apartment.

After I unpacked, she still hung around. I had this strange feeling that she wanted to get laid! (I guess one might consider it a sympathy fuck!) But my pride had been bruised!

I wasn't angry anymore, but I said she would have to get the divorce and pay for it. If she wanted the house, she would have to make the payments. I would sign it over to her and be done with it.

(Looking back "sometimes the fuckin' you get ain't worth the fuckin' you get!")

CHAPTER TWENTY-FOUR

What a Difference a Day (Job) Makes!

Time passed. All of my attention was now focused on the business. I picked up a couple of "bread and butter accounts" that took up the slack when things were slow. I worked with an interior decorator who would bring art prints to be framed for her clients and also a company that every two months ordered at least $2,000 worth of large posters to be framed and hung in their corporate offices.

During the time, I was with Vinton, his drummer and conductor, Lloyd Morales, was dating an attractive blonde lady whose name was Jan Moore. They eventually married, and Carol and I attended the wedding. We became good friends and interacted socially.

Jan was an aspiring singer and longed to get into show business. She and Carol worked up a duo whereby they sang two-part harmony while Carol accompanied on the piano.

I helped them put together a demo tape and submitted it to several hotel/casinos in Las Vegas. One motel did give them a couple of weeks in the bar, and they did rather well.

Carol and I both knew Tony Zoppi, the entertainment director at the Riviera, so we played the tape for him. He liked it and booked them for four weeks at the Riviera. That was about the extent of the career for the duo.

Unfortunately, Lloyd got involved with drugs and became abusive. Eventually, he and Jan were divorced.

I lost touch with both of them until one day, several months after Carol and I were separated, Jan walked into my frame shop.

She was now in real estate and working at a new Century 21 office just three doors up the street from my shop.

It was nice to see her. We talked for about an hour, had some laughs, and discussed our divorces!

I had seen an ad in the paper that Oscar Peterson was appearing at the Universal amphitheater the following week. I really wanted to hear him, so I asked Jan if she would like to go. She thought that would be wonderful, so we made a date. Also on the show were the Singers Unlimited, an excellent vocal group. They did the second half of the concert, but I was very disappointed! They got into this new-age shit that left me cold. We left before they finished.

We had a bite to eat after the concert then stopped by my apartment; being adults, we . . . ! We seemed to get along, so we entered into a steady relationship.

Jan was doing very well in real estate, and I continued to struggle with the frame shop. I even tried a new location. A small house a few blocks away that had housed a rock climbing business became vacant, so I signed a year lease and moved in. I felt it had more curb appeal for an artistic endeavor than my previous location.

I transformed one of the rooms into a gallery. I negotiated with a wholesale company that supplied art prints, paintings, and posters on consignment. A year later, I had sold a grand total of three pieces of art.

Chatsworth, where my shop was located, was just not an artistic community. (It has since become the largest center for the production of porn movies in the country.) It didn't have a decent restaurant or even a movie theater. Northridge, the nearest community to the east, was much more upscale. It seemed as though people coming to the Valley from Los Angeles came as far as Northridge but went no farther west!

I finally gave up and sold the business for the price of what it took to pay off my suppliers and creditors to a young Chinese guy who had been working for me as an apprentice. The next seven years would become the darkest period of my life.

One day, after selling my business, I was looking through the classified pages of the newspaper and under Help Wanted saw an ad for an art director to manage a new gallery in Northridge. I figured, *What have I got to lose?* I called the number and made an appointment for an interview.

I met with the owner, told him about my framing business and art gallery. (I skipped the part about having only sold three pieces in a year!) But to my surprise, he hired me at $400 a week.

The owner was a wealthy businessman and avid art collector, who hoped to turn his hobby into a successful business venture.

The gallery was located in a row of new storefronts behind a Marie Callender's restaurant and parking lot. I assumed that the traffic from the restaurant would gravitate toward the gallery.

The gallery owner wanted to have a grand opening, so I hand addressed two thousand invitations to potential customers. The affair was catered with wine and hors d'oeuvres.

It is hard to believe, but not one person showed up! A portent of things to come.

For the next five months, I watched a steady stream of customers coming and going from Marie Callender's, never once looking in the direction of the gallery! Soon after, we closed.

One summer day, I stopped at a mini-mart for a cold soda and saw a large sign over a storefront that said Fast Frame-Custom Framing. Curious, I walked over to take a look. There was a sign in the window that said, "Wanted . . . Manager . . . Experienced."

I went in and met Ken, the owner. Fast Frame was a new franchise business that advertised quick service for picture framing. (Not always the case!)

It was a nice setup though. All new fixtures and equipment. I thought I could enjoy working there, especially when it meant a steady paycheck ($400 a week). Ken felt it would work out fine, so he hired me to start immediately.

The business was doing rather well, so Ken decided to open another shop in Pasadena. He worked it by himself for a while then had me going back and forth between the two shops. Pasadena was quite a haul from where I lived, which meant leaving earlier in the morning and getting home later at night.

I suggested he let me operate the Pasadena store full-time at an increase in salary, but he wanted to keep the status quo! After eight months, I moved on.

I managed another frame shop, this time in North Hollywood, at an increase in salary, but the owner was a real schmuck, so I left after six months.

Jan and I were still seeing each other daily and becoming closer. She was doing well in real estate, and I had this vision of us getting married (in certain ways, I'm old-fashioned) and both working together. (It seemed like a good idea at the time!)

We had a simple ceremony and then spent a few days on a honeymoon in Palm Springs.

Jan sold the small condo she owned so that we would have a little money, and we moved into a two-bedroom condo in Canoga Park.

Century 21 offered to pay for my training in real estate school so I could get my license. It took nearly a year. The first time I took the state test, I failed by two points. I had to take a refresher course and passed it on the second try. All this time, we were living on the small amount of money Jan had made from the sale of her condo plus my credit cards.

Real estate in California was just starting to decline, so Jan's business dropped off dramatically!

Up to this point, anyone in California could sell a house, but now, in 1988, the market had reversed.

Being a real estate agent is not easy. You can work your ass off dealing with buyers and sellers. Even when you think you have a deal, it can fall through before closing. The problem then was if you're hurting, you may have already spent the commission.

I grew to hate what I was doing, the cold calling, which meant going to the office at 6:00 p.m., opening the phone book, going down the list, and calling people to ask if they had any interest in buying or selling a home. The hang ups and insults became depressing!

My real estate career ended in less than six months!

One day, while watching television, I heard a commercial about a healthcare company that had a plan aimed at Medicare recipients.

If you were on Medicare and had parts A and B, you could get 100 percent coverage with no monthly premiums or deductibles.

Since I had my heart attack, I had lost my medical coverage through the musicians union, so this plan sounded interesting.

It was offered by a company called FHP (Family Health Plan) an HMO (Health Maintenance Organization). I know it sounded too good to be true, but I called the number on the screen and made an appointment for a representative to come to the house and explain it. At first, I was skeptical, but by the end of the presentation, I decided to enroll. It didn't cost me anything, and I could drop out at any time.

I said to the representative, "This must be an easy job, giving seniors a relatively free health plan." He said it wasn't as easy as it sounded. I asked him who I needed to contact to apply for a job. He gave me the phone number of his supervisor. I called the next day and made an appointment for an interview. I figured being a senior and belonging to the plan myself might give me an advantage with other seniors.

The job paid a small salary, plus a $10 commission on every senior you could sign up. I took a two-week training course and was assigned to an office in North Hollywood.

The main idea was to contact as many eligible seniors as possible. Sometimes through leads provided by the company or by buying commercial lists of prospective customers or, once again, cold calling #@^*//+! to set up appointments. There was also a monthly quota you had to meet. There would be a meeting every morning at 8:30 a.m. to report on how many appointments you had made the day before, how many seniors you signed up, and if not, why? I soon found out that dealing with seniors was not as easy as I had imagined although being one of them did help a little.

There were fifteen other reps in the office, all competing for the limited pool of Medicare recipients. I had never worked in an office before, so I was unaware of the petty bullshit that went on, but I soon learned.

I did fairly well for a while, but working on a commission basis barely provides a living wage.

I worked out of that office for about six months, and then one of the reps told me of another HMO-United Health Plan—that had a plan with better benefits that might be easier to sell and that they were looking to hire new reps. I interviewed and was hired. Their office in Van Nuys had only eight reps, much less competition.

I had kept a record of all the people I had signed up at FHP, so I began calling them to let them know of the better benefits offered by the United Health Plan. (I don't know if that was unethical or just business!) More than 90 percent disengaged from FHP and switched to United. I won an award for most productive rep, my first quarter! Once I had exhausted my FHP referrals, it was back to the scramble of trying to recruit new enrollees.

Six months later, I heard a rumor that FHP was doubling the basic salary plus paying $15 per enrollment. I called my old supervisor and asked about the possibility of returning to FHP. I was rehired and was assigned to an office in Reseda, which now employed twenty-five reps.

Soon, rumors began to circulate that FHP would be opening a new territory in Ventura county, which included Simi Valley. Up until now, there was no plan like FHP for seniors on Medicare in that area, which meant a bonanza for any rep lucky enough to be assigned to that office. We were all interviewed and, fortunately, I was picked to be transferred.

In the meantime, Jan and I left the condo and rented a two-bedroom house in Sylmar at $1,700 a month, which meant buying new furniture on the credit cards. Jan's car was a Volvo that had seen better days, so we bought a late-model Cadillac with payments of $500 a month.

My new office was in Oxnard in Ventura County, which now meant a lengthy commute from our home. The first few months, I averaged three to four appointments a day and signed up quite a few new members for FHP. Two of these appointments stand out in my memory.

I parked my car in front of an old stone house set back from the street. The front yard was overgrown with weeds, and a rusty gate hung on one hinge. I rang the doorbell and waited. A thin, raspy voice came from the speaker beside the front door, "Who is it?" "Mr. Campbell from FHP." The answer was, "Just a minute." The door was opened by an elderly gray-haired lady, who smiled and said, "Come in, please."

The interior of the house was very dark, and a musty odor permeated the air, a combination of neglect and decay. She led me into the living room, seated herself in a rocking chair while I sat on a velvet-covered sofa and placed my FHP material on an old wooden coffee table. I went through my whole pitch about the FHP Medicare plan, and when I finished, she said she would like to sign up. I said I needed to see her Social Security card and Medicare card. She handed me those cards then held out another one. "Is your plan anything like this one?" she asked. I looked at the card she handed me. It was an FHP membership card! She was already a member of FHP. (Sadly, sometimes the elderly will make an appointment just to have someone to talk to.)

Another appointment of note took me to a run-down trailer park, not a mobile home park, but a trailer park! I knocked on the screen door of a single wide unit. A tall man wearing blue jeans and an undershirt bellowed, "Come on in." I followed him into the kitchen where he said, "Let's sit here," indicating a round table covered with a plastic tablecloth and a fifth of Jack Daniels whiskey in the center. "How 'bout a drink?" (This was ten thirty in the morning!) "No thanks, I gotta drive." I laughed. I finished my presentation, and the guy said he wanted to sign up. Once I verify that they are eligible, I am required to place a call to an FHP phone bank where a voice-activated system asks the new enrollee several questions regarding their understanding of the plan and their agreement to join. There is no person on the other end of the line, just a voice that is activated to ask the next question once they answer the previous one. When we finished, my new customer said, "Hey, I got a buddy who might be interested in this.

He's a retired jockey, want me to call him? He lives just down the street."
I had time, so I said, "Sure."

Fifteen minutes later, this little man about four feet three inches tall opened the door. We shook hands, and I could smell that he was already half in the bag. He spotted the Jack Daniels and helped himself to a hefty shot. His friend kept telling him he should join up, so he said, "Where do I sign?" He was eligible, so I signed him up. I explained that he had to answer some questions on the phone, so I placed the call and handed him the receiver. He answered the first two questions then said into the phone, "Do you like horses?" After a short pause, said, "Hey! I asked you a question. Do you like horses? Why don't you answer me?" I tried to tell him he wasn't talking to anybody, but he kept on. "What the hell's the matter with you?" After a short pause he said, "Aw, fuck you!" and hung up.

About this time, I began to have a problem with frequent urination. I would be driving to an appointment in the Valley, and by the time I got there, the first thing I had to ask was, "May I use your bathroom?" It rapidly got worse, causing me to see a proctologist. An examination revealed an enlarged prostate. He said he could reduce it with minor surgery. He also took a biopsy and said the result was negative.

The morning after the minor surgery, he casually told me, "By the way, you have prostate cancer." He had found it tucked away down under the prostate that the biopsy had missed. I was rather stunned but said, "Well, what do we do now?" He said, "We have two choices. We can either treat it with radiation or remove the prostate through surgery." He explained one problem could be the possibility of damaging the nerves that controlled erectile function. I thought for a moment and decided I didn't want to walk around, knowing I had that cancer in there. "Let's take it out, Doc, I've fucked enough!"

After the prostate surgery, Jan and I took a short vacation to Mexico (paid for with credit cards). I returned to FHP while Jan still struggled with the deflated real estate market. Working at FHP seemed like a dead end. I was really unhappy, and eventually I quit. I had no idea what I would do, but I didn't seem to care. Somehow Jan got us involved in a psychological, self-help program called PSI (People Synergistically Involved), their motto "Changing the World One Person at a Time." The first four weeks session cost us $400 each. It was very interesting, and I seemed to be getting some benefit from it, so we decided to move onto the next five-week session at $500 each, which we could ill afford. This session was much more psychologically intense, I almost quit halfway through it.

I had gotten interested in a new hobby, working with stained glass. I took a beginner's class at a local glass shop, then more advanced lessons with a lady who owned a studio in North Hollywood. I set up a small workshop in our garage and spent most of my time there.

Within a year, I had maxed out my credit cards and had fallen deeper in debt. Jan exacerbated the problem with her habit of writing checks against an account in which she didn't know the balance (or want to know), sometimes incurring charges of over $100 a month because of returned checks.

I avoided answering the telephone because nine times out of ten it would be a creditor looking for back payment. I called the finance company and said I was returning the Cadillac because I could no longer afford the payments. Jan bought a used Jeep Cherokee. (Her credit was still okay.) The money problem was weighing heavily on me, so I decided to seek credit counseling. The counselor's advice was, in my case, bankruptcy! Jan didn't want any part of it. She refused to file jointly. After it was over, I felt a great sense of relief but also realized that my good credit had been damaged for at least the next seven years.

In October of 1991, I suggested to Jan that we spend Halloween weekend at Big Bear Lake, a place we had been to several times, and I liked it very much. Even though I knew we shouldn't, we scraped up enough money to rent a cabin for three days.

The first night in the cabin, Jan was skimming through a week-old newspaper and said, "Honey, Buddy Morrow and the Dorsey band are playing here tomorrow night at the community center, would you like to go?" I looked at the ad. It said $20 per person. I said, "Maybe we could stop by after dinner at the back door and say hello to Buddy."

By the way, we had a beautiful female pet Doberman we named Sachcha. We drove to the rear of the community center, and Jan said, "I better stay in the car with Sachcha, so why don't you go in and see Buddy." I said, "Okay, I won't be long."

Buddy was surprised to see me, gave me a big hug, and asked, "What are you doing here, are you working around here?" I answered, "No, Buddy, I'm not playing anymore, I'm just here for the weekend." He looked puzzled. "What do you mean you're not playing anymore?" I said, "I've been working for a healthcare company, a day job." "Are you happy?" he asked. "No, I'm miserable!" I answered laughingly.

"Look," he said, "we're off for the holidays, but we'll be going back out in February. Why don't you get your horn out and come on the road with me?" "I can't do that, Buddy, I'm married, and I feel like I should be at home." He handed me his card and said, "Here, stay in touch, okay?" I said it was good to see him and thanked him for the offer.

When we got back to our cabin, Jan asked, "What did Buddy have to say?" I told her about his offer to go on the road with him in February. "And what did you say?" she asked. I really didn't want to talk about it, so I just said that I couldn't do it, that I felt I should be at home. "Why? You're certainly no fun to live with the way you are now. I know you're unhappy not doing what you want." I said, "Are you serious, you really want me to go?" She gave me a kiss on the cheek. "I just want to see you happy again," she said. (I will always thank her for that.) The following Monday, I called Buddy and asked if the offer was still open. He said it was, offered me $500 a week, and would let me know the details after Christmas.

Remember, I hadn't touched my horn in seven years. Laying off for more than two days makes you feel as though you have to start all over. (The trumpet can be a bastard!) I knew I had three months to get ready and that it wasn't going to be easy. I am a firm believer that the universe provides. In seven years, I had not received one call from anyone pertaining to playing the trumpet. Then one day, a call from a complete stranger saying someone had given him my name and that I was a trumpet player. He asked if I could read music. I said I believed I could handle it. He told me he had a rehearsal band that met every Thursday at a senior center, and could I come to the next rehearsal.

When I got to the center, I noticed that most of the guys in the band would never see fifty again, but that didn't mean they weren't great players. I didn't know what to expect. I was very nervous, so I quickly sat down in the fourth chair in the trumpet section. My chops were pretty weak, and I hoped I wouldn't be embarrassed. The leader beat off the first arrangement, and it was god-awful!

The only professional was the lead alto player. The others in the band were rank amateurs. By the third week, I had moved up to the first trumpet chair. I could've sat in my living room practicing every day for months, but there's nothing as rewarding as playing in the section to get back into shape.

Jan and I were still having a hard time. We had fallen two months behind in our rent but, for the kindness of our landlord, were not evicted. Jan negotiated a deal with one of her real estate friends for a lease to buy a small house in Chatsworth that had been on the market for some time at a monthly payment we could afford. Gradually, that seven-year period was coming to an end. I looked forward to the new year. The year 1992 had to be better!

CHAPTER TWENTY-FIVE

On the Road Again

After we moved into the house in Chatsworth, Jan became involved with channeling and therapy working with crystals. She converted one of the bedrooms into a comfortable workroom with a massage table and soon actually began to attract a few clients. I never fully understood what she was doing, but I had decided that she could do her thing and I would do mine. It bothered me that she had left me to go through the bankruptcy alone.

I opened my own checking account and told her we would each be responsible for our own finances. In February of 1992, I packed my bag and my trumpet and flew to Ohio to join Buddy Morrow and the Tommy Dorsey Orchestra.

The bus picked me up at the airport then headed for the first gig fifty miles away. That first night when I got on the bandstand and took my seat in the trumpet section, I had a good feeling. I felt right at home. The only chair available to me was the fourth trumpet chair. Another guy had been hired to play lead (I don't remember his name), which was okay with me because I needed some time to build up my chops. He only lasted a few weeks anyway. Also in the trumpet section was a guy Lin Blaisdell who had been with Buddy Morrow since the fifties and had been on Buddy's hit recording "Night Train." He tipped the scales close to three hundred pounds!

The next lead player was a young guy from Tennessee named Mike Wyatt. As soon as I heard him play, I knew he had great potential but needed some seasoning. The second night on the job on one of the Dorsey standards, he decided to show off a little by playing the ending of the arrangement an octave higher. Annoyed, I leaned forward and said to Mike, "Hey, man, we don't do that here. Just play what's on the paper." I think I scared him. He answered, "Yes, sir!" I really had no business saying anything, but I knew Buddy Morrow wouldn't; he rarely criticized anyone.

One day while riding on the bus, I noticed Mike wearing a pair of earphones and listening to his CD player. I asked him what he was listening to. He said his favorite Dorsey record, "They Didn't Believe Me," an arrangement by Bill Finnigan. I said, "Oh Yeah! I remember that. I was the lead player on that record." His eyes grew wide. "Are you kidding? You really played lead on that record?" I told him all about it; how it had been recorded in Hollywood in 1952, the second week after I joined Tommy Dorsey. Mike developed into a fine lead player and stayed with Buddy Morrow for thirteen years.

Lin Blaisdell was quite a character. His seat on the bus was opposite Buddy's. There were no seats in front of his, just a rack that held the extra band jackets plus two of Lin's white (tattletale gray) shirts. He had a large plastic cooler that contained some of his prized possessions. A fifth of vodka, a large jar of peanut butter, a bottle of witch hazel, and other assorted sundries. Lin was very fond of sandwiches made up of Wonder bread, Velveeta cheese, and Spam. He even had a baseball cap with the word *Spam* embroidered on the front.

I have always been amazed at the fact that there were so few accidents involving band buses during the years that dozens of bands traveled across the country under the most trying conditions. Such as bad weather, driving hundreds of miles at night after the job with drivers pushing the limits of safety, and some buses that seemed to be held together with spit and glue. In all my years on the road, I was involved in only one.

It happened one afternoon on a highway outside of Bryant, Indiana. We were stopped on the road, waiting to make a left turn into a side road that led to Bear Creek Farms where we were to play two shows that day. Suddenly, *BAM!* We were hit in the rear by a flatbed trailer truck. Apparently, the driver of the truck didn't realize we were stopped, and then when he did, he swerved but too late. I was in the seat behind Buddy and just happened to be looking at Blaisdell when we were hit. Lin shot out of his seat like a cannonball, all three hundred pounds, and wound up in a pile of band jackets! Thankfully, neither Lin nor anyone else was hurt, but the sight of him flying out of that seat still makes me laugh. (The last time we played Bear Creek Farms was on the morning of September 11, 2001/. My roommate, Ted Thompson, and I were watching television in our motel room and were assured that the local Air National Guard was protecting Fort Wayne!

Buddy's piano player was also the road manager, a man with an acerbic disposition. He liked to puff the punk (smoke pot), which may have accounted for his Jekyll and Hyde personality. (All it ever did for me was make me horny, so I never smoked it outside of the bedroom.)

Playing fourth trumpet in the band is not the most rewarding position to be in, but if that's where you are, you should do it with an attitude that it's as equally important as any other chair in the band. (More good advice from my trumpet teacher.)

Most of the time, we played two-hour concerts with a dance job thrown in here and there. Soon after I joined the band, Buddy said he would like to feature me on the concerts and asked if I had a solo number I could do. I didn't have anything at that time, so I called my friend Walt Stuart, an excellent arranger, and asked him to write an arrangement for me. He came up with a beautiful rendition of "What's New," a song that had been recorded by one of my favorite trumpet players, Billy Butterfield.

One-nighters in themselves are tough enough without having to put up with the constant partying every night on the bus. The ringleaders included several guys from Buffalo, New York, led by the road manager. He had devised a "fine" system whereby anyone who was late getting on the bus was "cased," meaning that person had to buy a case of imported beer to be put on the bus. Of course, the Buffalo contingent comprised of the heaviest drinkers, mostly benefited from this system. Also, drinking and carousing caused them to get overheated, so the air-conditioning would be on full blast even in the middle of winter. The windows would be thick with frost even on the inside! I moved to the rear of the bus, nearer the engine to keep warm, but there was a hole in the floor that allowed cold air to rush in. I bundled up as best I could, but it wasn't much help.

These conditions, plus the fact that I wasn't sure what I wanted to do about my marriage, caused me a lot of unrest. After a confrontation with the road manager, I decided to leave at the end of the current string of one-nighters. In the fall of '92, I returned to California to inform my wife of my decision.

Over the years, I had stayed in touch with Lynn Roberts, my first wife, because of our children and because we were still friends. Lynn had purchased a beach house on Sunset Beach, North Carolina, and had invited Jan and I to spend a week there anytime we wished. We took her up on her offer one spring when we felt the need to get away from California for a few days. I was very impressed with the area around Sunset Beach, especially the quaint little town of Calabash on the border between North

Carolina and South Carolina. Also, Lynn's brother Al and his wife, Peggy, had been living in Calabash for several years.

By the time I got back to California, I had decided I didn't want to be there anymore. I did not want to go back to New York, Pittsburgh, or Orlando, so I chose Calabash, North Carolina. I felt badly about putting Jan in this situation. I told her I cared very much about her, but I wasn't in love, and I didn't want to hold her back from finding new happiness in her life.

Jan had a female lawyer friend who suggested that we file for a dissolution of the marriage. Because there were no children or property involved, and if after six months, neither party contested the application, the dissolution would be granted. We both agreed, and it was done.

I closed my checking account, bought a used Mercury station wagon, rented a U-Haul, packed a few belongings including the stained glass pieces I had made, and headed East!

CHAPTER TWENTY-SIX

Myrtle Beach, South Carolina (The Redneck Riviera) (Part One)

When I called Lynn to tell her I was moving to North Carolina, she offered to let me stay at her beach house until I could find an apartment. The trip from California took four days. It was slowed down somewhat by having to pull the U-Haul.

After a good night's sleep, I spent the following morning sitting on the deck of Lynn's beach house, looking at the ocean and reflecting on the decision I had made. I had no idea what I would do. I didn't know anyone in the area except Lynn's brother. I didn't know if I would ever play the trumpet again, and somehow I didn't seem to care. My credit was shot, so I had to figure out how to manage on Social Security and a small pension from the musicians' union. (After sixty-eight years as a professional, it has ballooned to $308.66 a month! Most musicians have no pension at all.)

Within a week, I found a one-bedroom furnished condo on the outskirts of Calabash for $400 a month. It had a screened-in back porch, which became a workshop where I could resume my hobby of working with stained glass.

One morning, I saw an ad in the local paper that the Glenn Miller Orchestra was giving a concert the next evening at an auditorium just north of Calabash. The leader of the Glenn Miller Orchestra, Larry O'Brien, was a close friend of mine, so I decided to drive to the auditorium to say hello. I found the stage door and went in.

Larry was happy to see me and asked if I was still living in California. I said, "No, I just moved to North Carolina two weeks ago." He said, "You must know Charlie Lee, he lives here, but he's subbing on trombone, just for tonight." He called Charlie over. "Charlie, you know Flea, don't you?" Charlie reminded me that we had played together a few times when Charlie Spivak had reunited his big band to celebrate yearly anniversaries at Ye Old Fireplace, a great steak restaurant in Greenville, South Carolina, where Spivak had become a permanent fixture (and where my dear friend Charlie Russo was murdered during a robbery at the restaurant).

When I told Charlie Lee that I was living in Calabash, he said, "Hey, man! We have a big band in Myrtle Beach that plays every Wednesday afternoon at a place called Night Moods. Why don't you come down next Wednesday and sit in?" On Wednesday afternoon, I showed up with my horn and was invited to sit in by the leader Dr. Asbury Williams, who was also the first trumpet player. The band was called Swing Time and consisted of five saxes, four trumpets, four trombones, bass, drums, and piano. The library contained a lot of Sammy Nestico and Dave Wolpe arrangements among others. Overall, it was pretty good with a weak spot here and there. I sat next to Dr. Williams and split the lead parts with him, but it soon became obvious that although he had all the enthusiasm in the world, he didn't have the chops or endurance to be a strong lead player. I was very impressed by Joe Long, the jazz tenor player; Tony Capolingua, the lead alto player; and Bill Gregory, who played nice jazz trumpet on occasion. I really had a good time that afternoon and hoped that I would be asked to sit in again some time.

The next morning, I received a phone call from Dr. Williams asking if I would like to join the band. I said I would, but since they already had four trumpets, I wouldn't want to put anyone out of the band. I knew all of these guys loved to play and weren't doing it for the money. (Ha!)

Doc Williams said that they had a meeting after I left, and everyone agreed that I would be added and that none of the other players would be let go. I thanked him and said, "See you next Wednesday."

I spent the remainder of that year playing with Swing Time and enjoying my hobby until I received a call from Buddy Morrow in early 1993, saying the Dorsey band had some nice upcoming dates. A one-nighter in Paris, France, two cruises, a three-and-a-half-week tour of Europe, a PBS television show pending, and would I like to come back? It sounded like it might be fun, so I put aside the negative feelings and rejoined the band.

CHAPTER TWENTY-SEVEN

The City of Light

The one-nighter to Paris turned out to be quite an experience. The engagement was a private affair hosted by a very wealthy Englishman who wanted to throw a party for his friends. He flew them in from all over Europe. The entertainment featured Buddy Morrow and the Dorsey band with guest Lynn Roberts and the once-popular Trini Lopez. (Remember him?) After an all-night flight, we arrived in Paris early in the morning and were bused to our hotel.

We didn't have rehearsal until the next day, so Buddy, his wife Carol, Lynn, and I decided to do a little sightseeing. We didn't have much time, so we thought the Eiffel Tower might be a good bet. There weren't too many tourists there that day, so the line to purchase tickets wasn't long.

I can understand why the Eiffel Tower is considered one of the wonders of the world, it is fascinating! I'm not too fond of heights, so we didn't go all the way to the top, just to the level just beneath it. The view overlooking Paris is breathtaking, and the history surrounding the tower can be felt while there. We had lunch at the tower restaurant then walked back to our hotel.

Buddy suggested that the four of us have dinner in the hotel dining room. The food was excellent, but when the check came, Buddy and I had a problem trying to decipher it. We looked at each other, and both had the same thought. Since the rooms were comped, why not just sign for it and see what happens. We never heard another word about it.

A rehearsal was called for three o'clock the next afternoon at the very famous Maxim's restaurant where the party was to take place. The walls were covered with beautiful French Impressionist murals. The bandstand was set up in front of huge windows, and a small dance floor occupied the center of the restaurant surrounded by tables and large booths. Trini Lopez acted as his own conductor, so Buddy sat in one of the booths listening and soon fell asleep.

We ran down Lopez's music for about an hour then took a fifteen-minute break. When we returned to the bandstand, Trini called up his big number, "La Bamba," which featured him on the conga drum. There wasn't much to the arrangement, just a bunch of repetitious phrases while he danced around pounding on the conga drum. For some unknown reason, he couldn't seem to find a tempo he was happy with, so he kept on starting and stopping, starting and stopping, annoying the band and especially the rhythm section.

After thirty minutes of this, Lynn Roberts walked up to the bandstand with her hands on her hips and said to Lopez, "How much longer will you be . . . . There are other people waiting here to rehearse!" He mumbled some kind of an apology and said, "Okay, I'm finished."

Maxim's provided dinner for the band, and the food was great. The party started at ten o'clock, so at ten, Buddy beat off the intro to "Opus No. 1." I happened to be looking at the center booth and spotted the former secretary of state Henry Kissinger. At the sound of the music, he turned his head with a huge scowl on his face and for the rest of the evening never looked at the band again. Lynn finished her portion of the show to polite applause. After ten minutes of Trini Lopez, no one was paying any attention to him. ("La Bamba" laid a big Le Bomba!) So much for my adventure in the City of Light.

CHAPTER TWENTY-EIGHT

On the Road Again . . . Again

Back on the bus after the quick trip to Paris meant more one-nighters through the summer into the fall. On November 1, we left for an eighteen-day tour of Europe that encompassed five countries: Germany, Belgium, Switzerland, Sweden, and Denmark. My roommate Frank McCallum and I got flu shots before we left, and while in Belgium, I came down with the worst flu I ever had.

We had a beautiful Mercedes tour bus with plush seats and a drink-dispensing machine that dispensed water, coffee, and tomato juice. Our driver spoke very good English. We worked every night and traveled during the day, so we really didn't get to spend much time in any one place. Sometimes we were put up in chalets or bed-and-breakfast-type places that were very nice except I never took to having lunch meat for breakfast!

We got to Berlin at four o'clock one afternoon, played a concert in front of eight thousand people that evening then left at 10:00 a.m. the next morning. The next night, we played at a jazz club that had no heat to an audience of eight people! One of the highlights for me happened in Sweden when Mike Wyatt and I found a store that sold nothing but Swiss Army knives. I came home with one that had rosewood handles and is not available in the United States.

On November 19, we flew to Fort Lauderdale and boarded the Royal Viking Sun, a beautiful cruise ship for a seventeen-day cruise from Fort Lauderdale through the Panama Canal and up to San Francisco. This was the first of at least fifteen cruises I have done with Buddy Morrow and the Dorsey band. The Norwegian line and the Crystal Cruise lines are the best.

We arrived in San Francisco on December 5 then proceeded to work our way back East. The PBS show had come through and was to be filmed and recorded on December 13 and 14 from the old Indiana Roof Ballroom in Indianapolis, Indiana, a ballroom I had played many years before with Tony Pastor, Charlie Spivak, and Tommy Dorsey. The show was to be called the *Tunes of Tommy Dorsey* featuring Buddy and the band, Lynn Roberts, Walt Andrus, and the Pied Pipers. Shirley Jones was the hostess.

I have seen several PBS big band specials, most of them corny, but this tribute to Tommy Dorsey was really excellent. Even though Buddy had a bad cold, he played Tommy solos to perfection. Lynn was sensational, as usual, both with her solo numbers and lead singing with the Pied Pipers. Walt Andrus, although a little nervous, gave a fine rendition of "Without a Song." Shirley Jones was a very pleasant and knowledgeable hostess.

Somewhere during the European tour, I had decided that, once again, I would get off the road, so I gave Buddy my notice, effective after the PBS show. The band had a month off, so I thought this would be a good time. (It would be five years until I joined the band again.)

CHAPTER TWENTY-NINE

The Redneck Riviera
(Part Two)

W hile I was away, several new theaters sprung up around Myrtle Beach, adding to the ones already established. The Carolina Opry, the Alabama, the Ronnie Milsap, and Dolly Parton's Dixie Stampede were all geared toward country—Western and bad rock. (The Dixie Stampede show recreated the Civil War!) Also, every show featured an Elvis Presley impersonator. Everyone thought Myrtle Beach would be the new Branson, a small town in Missouri with multiple theaters that had become very successful. Myrtle Beach had a hundred golf courses and, of course, the beach itself.

One of the new theaters, the Palace, did bring in better, upscale entertainment, opening with Kenny Rogers then Johnny Mathis and later Steve and Eydie. Most of the guys from the Swing Time band played those shows. Although the theater did pretty good business, it couldn't sustain providing that level of high-priced entertainment. (The shitkicker shows did great though!)

Lynn Roberts had been living in Greenwich Connecticut while spending ten years performing with Benny Goodman and five years with Harry James. Television and radio commercials were now being produced by twenty-three-year-olds who were not about to hire a fifty-eight-year-old singer, no matter how good she was. We had stayed close over the years, so I was pleasantly surprised when she told me she was considering moving to North Carolina to be near her brother and also closer to her beach house on Sunset Beach. She bought a lovely two-bedroom condo in a marina in

Little River, South Carolina, halfway between Calabash and Myrtle Beach. The guys in Swing Time loved it when, on occasion, she would sing with the band at our Wednesday-afternoon gig. We also did several concerts combining the Swing Time big band with the Long Bay Symphony and featuring Lynn. Every concert was sold-out, which is unusual for a local symphony orchestra.

Several of the new theaters started booking production shows. The first one I did was called Hollywood Superstars featuring celebrity look-alikes such as Michael Jackson, Marilyn Monroe, Garth Brooks, Liza Minnelli, Tom Jones, and Barbra Streisand, plus a line of chorus girls and a seven-piece band. (It wasn't great, but it was kind of fun.)

When Superstars closed, I made a direct segue into another theater and a variety show called *From Nashville to Broadway*. A husband-and-wife team that had worked on cruise ships owned and produced it. The first half featured country and Western music, then after intermission, our eight-piece band, dressed in white tuxedo jackets, opened the second half with a condensed version of "The One O'clock Jump" with a bass player who thought time (rhythm) was a magazine! (I assume we were supposed to represent the swing era.)

The Broadway portion included an excerpt from the show *Music Man* whereby we had to march around the theater wearing heavy marching band costumes loaded with bugle beads and playing "Seventy-six Trombones"!

The finale of the show was a production number from *Les Miserables*. The music was on a soundtrack, so the musicians became actors and participated in the chorus. The owners had envisioned this show running for years, but dwindling attendance (even though we had an Elvis impersonator) soon indicated the inevitable. I didn't make it till the end. I quit after seven months.

It was now 1996, thirteen years since I had my heart attack in California. I had begun walking two miles every morning, rain or shine, and swam twelve laps in the condo-complex pool every afternoon, weather permitting. One day in early July, I went to the pool for my daily swim. After four laps, I had to stop. I was exhausted and breathing heavily. I had no chest pain, but I knew something was not right. My doctor recommended a stress test, and results showed that I had six blockages in my arteries. After consulting with the surgeon, it was decided that I was a stent candidate, despite my age, for bypass surgery. The five-way bypass operation went well. Lynn and my ex-sister-in-law Peggy nursed me back to health. Within five weeks, I was playing Kenny Rogers's return engagement at the Palace. (Albeit on third trumpet!)

Andrew Thielen, a drummer with the Swing Time band for a short while, wanted to start his own band and asked me to help put it together. He bought a bunch of published arrangements, music stands, and fancy vests as uniforms. We rehearsed, and it soon became somewhat decent. Andrew booked the band into several local pubs at cheap money just to have some place to play. We started out as a swing, dance band, but little by little, Andrew turned it into a commercial venture, sometimes featuring as many as four singers, funny hats, and big band rock arrangements. We made a CD and a television special for PBS South Carolina television. Andrew and I didn't agree on the direction he was going, so we parted. I have to give him credit though. He is a hustler and, after ten years, works consistently in the surrounding states. We are still friends.

The following year, the Palace Theatre presented a variety show called *Razzle Dazzle* starring Debbie Boone (Pat Boone's daughter) and Barry Sullivan of *The Brady Bunch* TV show. It did mediocre business until a hurricane damaged the rear of the theater, forcing it to close. (We never did get paid for the last weeks' work!)

CHAPTER THIRTY

In the Loop (and the Front Seat)

From 1998 and into 2000, I somehow wound up back with Buddy
Morrow and the Dorsey band. The cruise ship *Norway* showcased big band
cruises several times a year; one that we did featured the Dorsey band,
the Guy Lombardo band, the Glenn Miller band, and the Benny Goodman
band under the direction of Terry Meyers.

On the first day out, the cruise director asked for a meeting of the
bandleaders and their road managers. Buddy's road manager did not
attend; in fact, except for his time on the bandstand, he was nowhere to
be found. This infuriated Buddy, and after the cruise, during one of the
one-nighters, he called me to his room to tell me that this incident, on
top of others that had been building for some time, convinced him to
terminate the road manager. He then offered me the job. My first reaction
was to say, "No, thanks," but then I began to think about the perks. A
monetary increase, my own room paid for, the front seat on the bus, plus
having access to the inner workings of the band. I said yes. And Buddy
said, "Good!"

My duties included hiring musicians, booking accommodations on
the road, working out routes with the bus driver, contacting the clients
and collecting the check before each venue, and firming up details such
as arrival times, stage setup, food for the band, and sound check for the
vocalist. Some places had no sound system, so we used our own that was
carried on the bus. We had a month off during the holidays, so I called the
ex-road manager and asked if he would be kind enough to give me the list
of musicians and motels he had accumulated. His answer was, "I threw
all that shit away."

My first gig as road manager was the 2001 Inaugural Ball in Washington DC, celebrating the election of President George W. Bush. I had previously played for two inaugural balls; one with Sammy Kaye for President Nixon and one with Les Brown for Ronald Reagan. Inaugural balls are a pain in the ass not only because of the tight security, but because of the idiots who schedule the entertainment. They give you a timeline such as begin playing at seven three until seven fifty-two then start again at eight thirteen until eight forty-three. None of which ever goes off as planned.

I started putting the band together, and the first musician I called was Ted Thompson from Greensboro, North Carolina, a baritone saxophone player I had met on the cruise ship *Norway* where he was playing with the Guy Lombardo band. Ted told me it had always been his dream to play with the Tommy Dorsey Orchestra. He is a fine baritone player and in another time and place could have been with the original Dorsey band. Ted has been with Buddy Morrow and this Dorsey band for the past eight years and has become a very close friend. (We BS on the phone several times a week.)

After the Washington gig, we were scheduled to fly to Natchez, Mississippi and get on the *American Queen* riverboat for a cruise down the Mississippi River. When I awoke that morning and looked out the hotel window, I saw it had begun to snow. I had arranged with the inaugural transportation office to have a bus sent to the hotel at 10:00 a.m. to take us to the airport. When it arrived, I saw that it was a small school bus barely large enough to accommodate all of our guys and equipment. By now it was snowing heavily, and I was concerned that we might not make it out of Washington. We piled into the bus, got to the airport, took off in the foul weather, and made it to Natchez.

As road manager, I decided to do away with the "case" rule. I believe men should be treated as adults and not children to be punished.

Four years later, we played for President Bush's second inaugural, this time in a different auditorium but, as usual, a total fiasco! First of all, security would not allow our bus to get within two blocks of the auditorium, so we had to walk on icy sidewalks, carrying our horns and equipment to the building. Inside was a large dance floor between two bandstands—one for us and the other for a five-piece rock group that was louder than us even though we had seven brass! The brilliant schedule we were given had both bands playing at the same time. Unbelievable!

Another pet peeve of mine is having to pack a tuxedo for a three-week tour when only one night might be a formal affair, or on cruise ships during a seventeen-day cruise, at least two or possibly three nights are designated formal. The captain's welcome-aboard party and the captain's farewell party. (He probably hates it as much as I do.) Ordinarily we wear dark blue blazers and gray slacks, white shirts and matching ties. Blue and gray. (We call it our Civil War outfit.)

During the time I was with Tommy Dorsey, a priest, a close friend of the Dorsey family, we called him Father Jiggs, would join us on the road and ride the bus. He would remove his white collar and dress in sport shirts.

There are certain people who just love to be around big band musicians. With Buddy Morrow and the Dorsey band, a jolly gentleman Dr. Gail Burrier would join us on the road three or four times a year. He had his own seat on the bus, behind Buddy, and never seemed to mind the long trips. When Doc showed up, he came prepared. He always brought three or four cases of bottled water and bags filled with candy and cookies. He also joined us on several cruises with a lady friend (usually one of his nurses). He would sit through the band's performance night after night and always seemed to enjoy it.

A few months after my bypass surgery, my youngest daughter Juda Lynn and her husband John said they needed to buy a property that would help give them some tax relief; someplace I would like to live, pay whatever rent I could afford, and take care of it for them. I finally settled on a brand-new condo complex under construction in Little River just a few miles from where I was now living. I would go there every other day to watch the progress as it was being built. I picked a two-bedroom, two-bath unit with an enclosed back porch overlooking the ninth hole on a golf course, on the second floor of a three-story, nine-unit building.

The first three years I lived there was great. Then the unit above me was then sold to a woman who lived in New York, an absentee landlord who rented to anyone with the first month's rent. Most of the time they were eighteen- to twenty-year-old airheads with boom boxes that rattled my ceiling because of the garbage they listened to. I complained to the condo association but to no avail. It was also getting harder for me to climb the two flights of stairs with my luggage, coming home after a road trip.

I told my daughter I was no longer happy living there, so she asked if I would mind if they put the condo up for sale since it actually hadn't helped much with their tax problem and that they would help me get a place of my own.

In the meantime, Lynn Roberts had married Lewis Hankins, a gentleman she met while doing a show on the Mississippi Queen riverboat.

Lewis, made up and dressed in the image of Mark Twain, did a show based on the life and wit of the great humorist and also gave lectures about the Mississippi River to the passengers. (She can tell you more about it when, hopefully, she writes her own book.)

I put a down payment on a lot in a nice mobile home community called the Village at Calabash, just a mile from my friend Patti Lewellyn's stained glass shop and soon found a good deal on a roomy four-bedroom, double-wide unit. My daughter Juda Lynn helped me with the down payment, and because I was now creditworthy, I had no problem getting a mortgage.

I spent 2004 and 2005 back and forth with Buddy and the band. We were scheduled to appear for a week at Busch Gardens in Tampa, Florida, when Buddy developed a serious medical problem. Buddy's wife, Carol, who was now booking and managing the band, asked me to take over as leader until Buddy got better. I knew I could handle it musically, and as far as being an MC, I borrowed some of Buddy's patter and eventually added my own.

For the past year, I had been doing my own feature spot in the concerts, combining some stale jokes with the singing and playing of my own arrangement, "I Can't Give You Anything but Love, Baby."

I felt very comfortable in front of the band. The guys in the band felt comfortable also as they let me know on several occasions. To offset the fact that Buddy wasn't there, I would announce that like Buddy, I was one of the few remaining original members of the Tommy Dorsey Orchestra. My credibility was established, and everyone was satisfied. I continued fronting the band, even during several cruises, until Buddy recovered. (At age eighty-nine, he is back as the leader.)

In February of 2005, we were booked on the Crystal Cruise line ship *Serenity* commemorating the hundredth year of Tommy Dorsey's birth and to kick off a new biography of Tommy written by Peter Levinson. With us were Lynn Roberts, Buddy De Franco, and Louis Bellson. It was a fun trip capped off with a great concert featuring the band, Lynn, Buddy De Franco, and Louis. De Franco played as well as ever. (His cabin was next to Lynn's, and she told me she could hear him practicing several hours a day.) Louis Bellson had become stricken with Parkinson's disease, and it was sad watching him try to play the drums; but he has remained the sweet man he always was.

After returning home from the cruise, a new change was blowing in the wind!

CHAPTER THIRTY-ONE

Closing Theme

The year 2005 was to become a significant year. Dates for the Dorsey band were few and far between, averaging only to two or three a month, with a cruise, using a seven-piece band, thrown in on occasion.

With all this free time, I flirted with the idea of doing my own CD, so I began picking the tunes and writing the arrangements. Years ago, I had bought some records featuring Ziggy Elman on trumpet with four saxes and a rhythm section. I decided that was the combination I would use. I asked Lynn Roberts if she would sing a couple of songs on the album. She said, "Of course." So I got to work.

After Lynn and her husband Lewis married, they bought a home in Carolina Shores just two miles from my mobile home. Lewis and I developed a good relationship, and so I talked or saw one or the other of them almost every day.

Our good friend Bob Alberti and his wife, Shirley, had moved from the rat race in California to Hilton Head Island, South Carolina, in 1993. Bob had called me once or twice to play in a big band concert sponsored by the Hilton Head Symphony Orchestra, so I was a little familiar with the area.

Apparently, Bob called Lynn one day to tell her that he and Shirley were selling their house on Hilton Head Island and moving to Sun City Hilton Head built by developer Del Webb, an over-fifty-five retirement community a few miles in on the mainland. He described how wonderful it was and said she and Lewis should come and check it out. During the discussion about the possibility of moving, Lewis said, "What will we do about Flea?" Lynn was surprised but then said, "I don't know. Let's ask him."

She called me and asked, "How would you feel about living in Hilton Head?" My answer was, "Oh no, I could never afford to live there." She told me about the discussion with Bob and that she and Lewis planned to drive to Hilton Head the following weekend to attend a presentation given by Sun City, and would I like to go along. I said, "Sure, it doesn't cost anything to look."

The following Friday, we arrived late in the afternoon and checked into the Hampton Inn close to the main gate at Sun City. We had dinner at a nearby restaurant, and since the presentation was not until ten o'clock the next morning, we decided to drive into Sun City and look around. It was beginning to get dark, so we couldn't see very much. I noticed how beautifully the grounds were landscaped; however, it was very quiet with only a few people strolling along the sidewalk or a golf cart driving by occupied by obviously senior citizens. My first impression was not favorable. When we got back to the hotel, we discussed how we felt about what we saw. My comment was, "I'm not sure I want to live with a bunch of old farts." We decided to wait until after the presentation the next day before making a judgment.

After a short orientation, we were taken on a tour of the facility. Everything looked different in the sunlight. Lush green foliage, sparkling lakes and ponds, and people jogging or walking their dogs. The model homes were very attractive and reasonably priced. We were shown the craft center, a well-equipped woodworking shop and model railroad layout, two fitness centers and swimming pools, two golf courses with restaurants right on the grounds; but what convinced me the most were the people we met who lived there and said moving to Sun City was the best thing they had done. We had dinner with Bob and Shirley that evening and told them we were seriously considering moving to Sun City. They were excited!

We returned home and started to devise a plan. Lynn would put both her beach house and Carolina Shores home up for sale, purchase two homes in Sun City, one for them and a smaller one for me. She was very generous in accepting my offer to pay the same amount of monthly rent as my mortgage payment. Of course, I also had to sell my home. I listed it with RE/MAX, sat back, and waited. The houses in Sun City wouldn't be available until the middle of 2006, so all these plans would have to come together at the right time. I decided to put off my plans for the CD until after the holidays.

Lynn received an offer almost immediately on her oceanfront beach house. Since there was no more beachfront property available on Sunset Beach, her house had increased in value to the point where she would be able to pay cash for both houses in Sun City with the profit she was sure to make from the sale. We made a trip to the Design Center at Sun City to pick out the amenities and upgrades Lynn wanted.

The house we picked for me is a lovely two-bedroom, two-bath, and two-car garage on a nice lot with a lagoon at the rear of the house. We added a garden room and a four-foot extension to the garage along with carpet, tile, and countertop upgrades.

In the spring, I finished the eleven arrangements of the songs I planned to use for the album then set about hiring the musicians. The sax section included Tony Capolingua on alto, Mike Duva on tenor sax, Ray Hutcheron on alto sax, and my friend Ted Thompson on baritone sax. My pal Joe Long provided all the wonderful tenor sax solos. I played the ensemble trumpet parts plus my own solos. For the rhythm section, I chose Judy Duva, Mike's wife and an accomplished arranger in her own right who helped me numerous times with my writing, on piano, Tom Hanlon on electric guitar, Don Mincher on bass, and a choice that gave me a great deal of pleasure—my grandson, sixteen-year-old Zachary Campbell at the drums. He played like a pro on the drum breaks I had written for him on Charlie Shavers's "Undecided."

Mike and Judy Duva graciously allowed us to rehearse in their home, and in July, we recorded the album in two sessions at a studio in Myrtle Beach. I overdubbed several of my solos that I wasn't happy with on August 25, 2006, my eighty-second birthday. (The album is titled *I'm 81 and Havin' Fun.*)

Also in the spring, Lynn had accepted offers on both her beach house and Carolina Shores houses. After being on the market for eleven months, I accepted an offer for my mobile home. Even after two price reductions, I realized a decent profit from the sale. My house in Sun City was ready for occupancy in August, so I moved in even though the closing date on my mobile home wasn't until September. Lynn and Lewis moved into their new house in October. Bob and Shirley Alberti lived about three blocks from us.

In May of this year, Buddy and the Dorsey band were scheduled for a three-week tour on the bus. I called Buddy and said I had had enough, I was getting off the road for good. (No one believed me, they had heard this dozens of times before, but this time I meant it.)

Now in 2008, my trumpet playing consists of playing three or four local Broadway shows a year at the Arts Center of Coastal Carolina on Hilton Head Island as part of a seven-piece pit orchestra.

I feel sorry for the thousands of musicians that have come after me and find it difficult to just play their instruments, make a decent living, and get a little respect and appreciation for their talent. (Many people think playing an instrument is just a hobby.)

I myself have been truly blessed. The young boy who sat in the front row at the Stanley Theater in Pittsburgh and dreamed about being up there on the stage, being part of that music, saw his dream come true.

That wonderful big band sound is almost gone, replaced by twanging, banging, and pyrotechnics! My friend Bob Alberti surmised, "Today's popular music just reflects the culture." I cringe when I hear the melody of the "Star-Spangled Banner" being butchered by some four-time Grammy winner, or walk into a local music store overflowing with guitars and say to the salesperson, "I'd like to buy a cup mute." And they answer, "What's that?" Or watch the closing credits in a movie or TV show where the music credits come long after the people who do the payroll, drive the limos, or supply the catering!

My trumpet has made me many friends—musicians I admired and respected and was humbly accepted as one of them. It also took me to places I never imagined I would see. (My only regret is that I never learned to play the piano.)

I have also been blessed with three remarkable children. My daughter Darla, a lovely, bright lady, still single (There are a lot of schmucks out there, Dad!), who has experienced a few bumps in the road, is now finding peace in her life through her faith. My son Daryl, who had the talent to become a professional musician playing the piano and writing beautiful music, decided to pursue a career that would provide more security and stability. At the age of forty-seven, he is entering law school in Seattle. My adorable and never-a-dull-moment daughter Juda Lynn has been happily married to her husband John for eighteen years. She has entered and completed numerous marathons and grueling iron man competitions across the country, which requires guts and commitment. I love and am extremely proud of each of them. My grandson Zachary, soon to enter a prestigious music school in New York City and who at age nineteen has already become a tasteful, professional, musical spirit. I know in my heart that he will play a very important part in keeping this music alive.

With regard to my affair with the trumpet, Dizzy Gillespie once said, "Some days you pick up the horn and everything is wrong, you can't do anything right, so the horn wins. The next day you pick up the horn and everything is beautiful, you can't do anything wrong, and you win; then you die, and the horn wins."

Just "DON'T BURY ME IN A TUXEDO!"

INDEX

A

AA (Alcoholics Anonymous) 69, 70
AF of M (American Federation of
    Musicians) 23
"Ain't She Sweet" 69
Albam, Manny 55, 80
Alberti, Bob 57, 134, 182, 185
Alberti, Shirley 182-4
albums 45, 110, 135, 184
"All That Glitters Is Not Gold" 43
All American 106
Allen, Gene 108
Ambassador Hotel 30
Americana Hotel 110
Amoroso, Johnny 74
Anderson, Cat 155
Andrus, Walt 174
Anna (drummer) 80
Anthony, Ray 68-9
Astor, Bob 25-6, 30
Atkinson, Jean 38
Atlantic City 30, 45, 138, 140
Aurex Jazz Festival 134

B

A Band 36, 39
Band of America 105
band, big 20, 23, 59, 76, 112, 129,
    137, 170, 176

Band of Renown 129, 133
Bartha, Alex 31
Barzie, Tino 48, 62-3, 65, 69, 73
Basehart, Richard 135
Bauwal, Fred 124
Baylis, Bob 35, 37, 39, 42, 45-6
B Band 35-6
Bellson, Louis 126, 181
Beneke, Tex 104, 122, 128-9
Bennett, Tony 81
Benzedrine 38
Berkeley's Jungle Gardens 22
Bibs Mosler 65
Bill Green's (club) 51
Blackton, Jay 108
Blaisdell, Lin 165-6
Bonfa, Luis 102
"Boogie Woogie" 124
Brad Hunt's Orchestra 47
Brauner, Buzz 74
Broadway 102-3, 106, 108, 110, 176
Brown, Les 129, 133, 153, 179
BTC (Basic Training Center) 34
Burnette, Smiley 58
Burrier, Gail 180
Butterfield, Billy 167

C

Café Rogue   43-4
California   65, 74, 78, 109, 113-4, 128,
    132-3, 154, 159, 167, 169, 176
  Anaheim   114-5
  Pasadena   158
Campbell, Juda Lynn   110, 180
Campbell, Catherine Wentz   13
Campbell, Chester Homer   13
Campbell, Dana Jack   14
Campbell, Darla Juda   101
Campbell, Daryl Jude   104
Campbell, Edwin Daryl "Flea"   9
  corporal   35
  divorce   126, 153, 155
  inaugural balls   179
  mobile home   115, 124, 154, 182
  prostate cancer   162
Campbell, Homer Ronald   14
Campbell, Ronnie   16-7
Capitol Theatre   17-8, 68
Capolingua, Tony   170, 184
Carbone, Vinnie   17, 62, 135
Carlan, Tommy   23
Carol (second wife of Flea)   138-9,
    153, 155
Carson, Johnny   114
Carter, Bob   56-7, 74
Castle, Lee   48, 74
Cavalcade of Bands   59
CCC (Civilian Conservation Corps)
    15
Cebek, Stan   47
Century Plaza Hotel   133
Charlie Spivak Orchestra   18, 41
Charlie's Tavern   43-4
Chatsworth   136, 157, 165
Cheese and Crackers Hagan   50
Cherb, George   64
Chester, Bob   26, 39

Chicago   76
Chicago (place)   42, 64
Chicago Theater   53
Childers, Buddy   61-2
"Chiribiribin"   129
"Christmas Song, The"   38
Clambake Seven   17, 74
Clarkson, Jeff   134
Clooney, Betty   38, 45
Clooney, Rosemary   45, 134
Club, the (establishment)   119
Cohen, Paul   73, 76, 101, 112
Collins, Pat   58
Conte, Richard   113
Contemporary Resort   123-5
Copacabana   11, 81-2
Costly, Clyde   20, 22
Count Basie   25
Cronk, Billy   74
Crosby, Bob   104, 115-6
Croydon Hotel   41
"Curtain Time"   55

D

Damone, Vic   81
"Dance Ballerina Dance"   120
Dancing Campbells   16, 18
Dark Orchid   135
Davey Millers   42
Davis, Mel   114
Daye, Irene   53, 56, 58
De Franco, Buddy   134, 181
Deauville Hotel   113
"Deep Purple"   21
Delugg, Milton   114
Dennis, Matt   45
Desmond, Johnny   44
DiMayo, Nick   62
Disney World   38, 124-7, 130
Disneyland   108-9, 114-5
Donahue, Sam   62, 115

Doran, Harry   37
Dorsey band   72
Dorsey Brothers Encore   75
Dorsey, Chipper   71
Dorsey, Jimmy   21, 57
Dorsey, Tess   73
Dorsey, Tommy   17, 31, 61, 64, 85,
    119, 124, 166, 174, 180-1
  funeral service   11
  sexual preference   72
  theme song   12
Droun, Elmer "Bunny"   49
drummer   35, 49, 54, 65, 102, 137,
    156, 177
DuBarry Was a Lady   75
Duke Ellington Orchestra   155
Durante, Jimmy   81
Durso, Mike   82, 102
Duva, Judy   184
Duva, Mike   184

E

"East of the Sun"   49
Eberle, Ray   129-30
Eberly, Bob   74
Edgewater Beach Hotel   64
Edson, Stan   118, 124
Eldridge, Roy   33
Elliot, Baron
  Stardust Melodies   48
Elliott, Baron   47-9, 51
English, Charlie   44
Enright Theater   17
Europe   170, 173
"Every Cat Has Nine Lives"   59

F

Faber, George   37
Father Jiggs   180
Femanella, Artie   124
FHP (Family Health Plan)   159-62

Fiengold, Jay   107
Finnigan, Bill   64, 73
Fiorello!   103-4
Flannagan, Ralph   45
Florida   38, 111, 113, 121, 123, 125,
    181
  Miami   81, 112-3
  Orlando   38, 121, 123-7
Flory, Med   34
Flying Leathernecks   113
Foy, Jimmy   124
Frank, Irving   37, 39
Freedomland   107
French, Red   49
Fresk, Babe   61
Frosk, John   75-6, 102
Frost, Wallace   20
Fuzzy Knight   64

G

Garner, Errol   36
Garner, Linton   36
Gazzo, Conrad   64
Gene, Autry   15, 58
Georgie Auld   134
Gershwin, George   33
"Getting Sentimental over You"   12
Geyer, Bobby   42
"Ghost Riders in the Sky"   120
Gibling, Howard   73-4
Gilbert, Billy   58
Gillespie, Dizzy   36, 185
Gleason, Jackie   76
Glenn Miller Orchestra   101, 169
Glover, Mary   27
Glow, Bernie   113
Goldstein, Chuck   101, 110
Goodman, Benny   107-9, 175, 178
Grady, Eddie   65
"Green Eyes"   74
Greene, Bob   20

Gregory, Bill 170
Gregory, Dan 43, 45
Groom, Joe 80, 113
Gubin, Sol 110
"Guys and Dolls" 109
Guzikoff, Saul 108

H

Hackett, Bobby 22, 126
Hale, Alan 35
Hampton, Lionel 25
Hanlon, Tom 184
Heinlein, Glenn 33
Henderson, Jimmy 74
Heston, Charlton 38
Hildegard 132
Hilton Head Island 184
Hines, Mimi 125
HMO (Health Maintenance
      Organization) 159-60
Hollywood 75, 166
Honeymooners, The 76
Hope, Bob 134
Hotel del Coronado 133
Hotel Fourteen 81-2
Hotel Pennsylvania 43-4
Hotel Syracuse 67
Hudson, Dean 26, 39
Hunt, Brad 47
Hutcheron, Ray 184
Hutton, Ina Ray 35

I

"I Can't Give You Anything But Love,
      Baby" 181
"I Wish You Love" 119
"If the Japs Only Knew What Our
      Arranging Staff Could Do" 37
"In Flew the Flea" 53, 59, 60
"I've Got Five Dollars" 55

J

Jack (uncle of Flea) 13-4, 23, 25, 35
"Jada" 121
Jamaica 116-8
James, Harry 20, 129, 175
Japan 134-5
"Japanese Sandman" 50
jazz club 126, 173
Jazz Messengers 134
Jenny 108-9
Jimmie Lunceford Orchestra 47
jingles 101
John (husband of Juda Campbell)
      180, 185
Jones, Shirley 174
"Jukebox Saturday Night" 128

K

Kail, Jerry 102
Kate (aunt of Flea) 13
Kaye, Sammy 104, 114, 179
Kelly, Paula 128-9
Kelly's 44
Kelton, Lee 47
Ken (owner of Fast Frame) 158
Kids of the Kingdom 131
Kincaid, Dean 73, 124
King Cole Trio 33
King, Wayne 104, 121
King, Peggy 58
King, Tommy 132
Kirby, John 64
Klemeck, Victor 22
Kramer, Don 133

L

"La Bamba" 172
"La Cucaracha" 119
Lady in Cement 112
Lake Tahoe 74, 138

Lambert, Fred   36
Lamond, Don   124
Las Vegas   71-2, 78, 139, 153, 155-6
Laubach, Jack   83
Lavalle, Paul   105
Lee, Charlie   170
Lenza, Joe   104-5
Les Brown band   113, 129, 133, 135-7
Les Miserables   176
Lesko, Johnny   102-3
Lewellyn, Patti   181
Lewis   181-2, 184
Liberace   120-1, 124
Lieutenant Harry Taylor   35-6
Lo Pinto, Frank   81
Local 802   60, 81, 102
Logan, Josh   109
Lombardo band   178-9
Lombardo, Guy   39
Long Island   11, 45-6
Long, Joe   17, 170, 184
Longo, Jimmy   112
Lopez, Trini   172
Los Angeles   132, 139, 155
Lost Weekend   70
"Love for Sale"   107
"Lulu's Back in Town"   17
Lunceford band   47, 111
Lunceford, Jimmie   21, 47
Lynn, Tommy (Leonnetti)   41, 53, 55

M

Mabley, Moms   50
Maguire, Larry   130
Major Bowes Amateur Hour   17
Maltby, Richard   31, 104, 115
Mangano, Mickey   75
Marie (chorus girl)   50
Marie Callender's (restaurant)   158
Marino, Barney   35
Markham, "Pigmeat"   50

Marowitz, Sam   123
Marshall, Billy   67
Martin, Tony   38
Maxey, Virginia   41, 45
May, Billy   104, 112
McGovern, Maureen   135
McKinley, Ray   104, 122-3, 129
McRae, Gordon   135
Medicare   159-61
Miller, Glenn   20-1, 34, 122, 128-30, 178
Mills, Jackie   65
Mincher, Don   184
"Mississippi Mud"   69
Modernaires   101, 128-9
Monroe, Vaughn   66, 104, 119-20
Moody, James   36
Moore, Jan   156
Morrow, Buddy   17, 59, 78, 104, 110, 116-7, 124, 163, 165-6, 170, 173-4, 178-9, 181, 184
Morrow, Carol   117
Motcalm, Russ   56
Mr. Schiller (drugstore owner)   21
Mr. President   106
Music Man   176
Music with Mary Martin   102, 109

N

From Nashville to Broadway   176
NBC   114, 134
NCO (Noncommissioned Officers) 35-6
Negri, Joe   48
Nestico, Sammy   48, 135, 170
New Penn   22
New York   17, 32-3, 185
   Queens   84, 103, 110
   world's fair   105
Nichols, Bobby   66
"Night Train"   117

North Carolina
  Calabash 167-70, 176, 181
  Fayetteville 58
North Dakota 138, 153
North Hollywood 138-9, 153, 158,
    160, 163
Norway 178-9
Nottingham, Jimmy 108

O

O'Brien, Larry 169
O'Connor, Donald 38
O'Connell, Helen 21, 74, 127
O'Connor, Donald 38
"Off We Go into the Wild Blue
    Yonder" 33
O. Henry Hotel 40
Ohio
  Youngstown 26, 51-3
Oklahoma 114-5
Oliver, Sy 73
one-nighters 43, 48, 53, 64-6, 76-7,
    114, 119-20, 167, 170-1, 173
"One O'clock Jump, The" 81, 176
"Open the Door, Richard" 50
orchestra 21, 23, 25, 47
ORD (Overseas Replacement Depot)
    38-9
"Over the Rainbow" 20, 23

P

Palmer, Arnold 125-6
Panico, Corny 45
Panther Room 39, 41
Parade Rest 36
Paris 170-1, 173
Parks, Bert 84
Pastor, Stubby 42
Pastor, Tony 31, 39, 53, 174
PBS 135, 174
Pell, Dave 26

Pennsylvania 13-4, 49, 61, 114, 137
"Peppy Pirates, The" 48
Perilli, Johnny 102
Perry, Dick 101, 114
Peterson, Oscar 157
Piccadilly Hotel 83
Pied Pipers 174
Pittsburgh 14, 17, 27, 47, 66, 132,
    168, 185
Plaza Hotel 102
Podell, Jules 81-2
"Polish Prince, The" 137
Polk, Gordon 69, 71, 75, 128
Polk, Vernon 128
Poodle Lounge 112
Powell, Al 47, 51
Princess Anne Hotel 23
Pring, Bob 37-9, 41-2, 45
Privan, Bernie 34
PSI (People Synergistically Involved)
    162
Pssarella, Lou 22
Pulley, B. S. 113
Pupa, Bill 21

R

"Racing with the Moon" 120
radio band 34-5, 37, 39
Razzle Dazzle 177
Reilly, Luke 49, 50, 52
rhythm section 124, 182, 184
Rich, Buddy 78
Ricky, Bobby 54-5, 102
Rise and Fall of the Third Reich, The
    104
Riviera Hotel and Casino 137, 156
road manager 43, 45, 55, 104, 118,
    167, 179
Roberts, Lynn 11, 58-9, 66-7, 69-72,
    74, 76, 78, 80, 83-5, 101, 110,
    112, 167, 171-2, 174-6, 180-4

Rogers, Eileen 59
Roosevelt Hotel 69, 71
Russo, Charlie 51-2, 54-6, 58-9

S

Sachcha (pet Doberman) 163
San Francisco 133, 173-4
Saxony Hotel 78
Schatsberg, Cy 35
Schmidt, Kloman 49, 50
"Seventy-six Trombones" 176
Severinsen, "Doc" 114
Shavers, Charlie 20, 62-3, 66, 184
Sherman Hotel 39, 43
Shoreham Hotel 124
Silent night 135
Sinatra, Frank 83, 112-3
Singers Unlimited 157
"Sioux City Sioux" 43
Skyscraper 106
Small, Danny 25
Small, Hy 102
"Someone to Watch over Me" 74
Song of the South 45
Sonju, Russ 54
South Carolina
   Charleston 22
   Myrtle Beach 17, 169-70, 175-6,
      184
Spain
   Madrid 138
Spano, Billy 124
Spitalny, Maurice 47
Spivak, Charlie 59, 62, 67, 69, 170
Spivak's band 51, 67-8, 74, 102,
      105, 121
Stage Show 76
Stanley Theater 23, 66, 185
Star Dreamers 57
"Star-Spangled Banner" 185
"Stardust" 129

Statler engagement 76-7, 84
Statler Hotel 11, 73-7, 84
Steel Pier 31, 138
Steinke, Mickey 37
Stone, Butch 130, 133, 153
Stonzek, Morris 104
Sun City 183-4
Sunset Beach 167, 175, 183
Supersax 34
Swanson, Bob 101
Sweden 173
Swing Time 170, 175-7

T

Taft Hotel 58, 67, 69
"Tangerine" 74
Tavorian, Tak 48
Taylor, Harry 35
Teentimers 44
television 49, 175
Tennill, Toni 135
Terry, Clark 114, 126
"That Old Feeling" 42
"That's a Plenty" 16-7
"There I Said It Again" 120
"There's No Tomorrow" 57
"They Didn't Believe Me" 166
Thielen, Andrew 177
Thompson, Ted 166, 179, 184
Tommy Dorsey Orchestra 17, 48,
      165, 179, 181
Tonight Show, The 114
Tony Pastor band 31, 39, 41-2, 44,
      53, 174
Top of the World 123, 125-7, 129,
      131
Traxler, Gene 124
Traynor, Tom 128-9
Tunes of Tommy Dorsey 174
Tunetimers 41

U

"Undecided" 184
United Health Plan 160
USO (United Service Organizations)
   36-7

V

Vincent Lopez Orchestra 58
Vine Lodge Motel 62-3
Vinton, Bobby 137, 153-6
Vinton, Dolly 140
Voltair, Paul 124

W

WAC (Women's Army Corps) 34
Warm Friends Tavern 42
WCAE 47, 132
West Coast 63-4
West Palm Beach 115-6, 120
Wetzel, Ray 63
Wexler, Moe 35
"What's New" 167
Wheel Café 50, 52
"Whiffenpoof Song, The" 48
"White Christmas" 118
Whitlinger, Freddy 49
Wilkins, Ernie 73
William Penn Hotel 25
Williams, Cootie 108
"Without a Song" 174
Wofford Beach Hotel 78
Wolpe, Dave 170
Wuest, Harry 104, 114-5, 117-20,
   123, 129
Wyatt, Mike 165, 173
Wynton Marsalis 135

Y

Yannon, Buddy (Iannone) 17, 53
"Yes Sir, That's My Baby" 13

Z

Ziggy Elman 63, 182
Zoppi, Tony 156